FOUNDING FATHERS OF SOCIOLOGY

FOUNDING FATHERS OF SOCIOLOGY

Comte, Marx, Spencer, Durkheim and Weber

SUJIT KUMAR CHOUDHARY

MANOHAR
2025

First published 2025
First eBook edition 2025

ISBN 978-93-6080-329-2 (hardbound)
ISBN 978-93-6080-477-0 (ebook)

Published by
Ajay Kumar Jain *for*
Manohar Publishers & Distributors
4753/23 Ansari Road, Daryaganj
New Delhi 110 002

Printed and bound by CPI Group (UK) Ltd, Croydon, CRo 4YY

Dedicated to my Babuji
Late Krishna Mohan Choudhary

Contents

Preface

The book *Founding Fathers of Sociology: Comte, Marx, Spencer, Durkheim, and Weber* is a significant collection of the writings on Auguste Comte, Karl Marx, Herbert Spencer, Emile Durkheim, and Max Weber. They are called classical thinkers of sociology who led the foundation of the discipline. In writing, I consulted many original classical works on the founders of sociology in general and some of the commentaries available on these thinkers. However, this became possible only because I was a student at the Centre for the Study of Social Systems, Jawaharlal Nehru University, New Delhi, during 1999-2008, from where I completed MA, MPhil, and PhD in Sociology.

The book concentrates mainly on the biographical sketch, approaches, perspectives, theories, methods, and methodology of these sociological thinkers. However, the discipline of sociology is much older than many of its students and teachers thought about it. After the French Revolution, sociology had its roots when political conflict, rapid urbanization, and social turmoil convulsed European societies. Intellectuals sought to explain the bewildering chaos and the new possibilities around them. Auguste Comte (1798-1857) was the first to use the word 'sociology' in his six-volume work *Positive Philosophy*, first published in 1842. Sociology can best be understood after a study of many thinkers as different perspectives and theories collectively comprise our understanding of the social world.

My intention in writing this book is to provide lucid, precise, and easy-to-understand classical thinkers and their theories of sociology to the students, academicians, and researchers of sociology and other disciplines of social sciences. I believe this book would reach every level of students, teachers, researchers, and academicians. In this book, I have tried to maintain the originality of the thought of these thinkers in simple language. The book is divided into five chapters: Auguste Comte, Karl Marx, Herbert Spencer, Emile Durkheim, and Max Weber.

Chapter One, 'Auguste Comte, 1798-1857', covers a wide range of theoretical analyses, including establishing a separate discipline of social sciences called 'Sociology'. Chapter two, 'Karl H. Marx, 1818-83', deals with theoretical perspectives of society and the ground reality of every type of society. The third chapter, 'Herbert Spencer, 1820-1903', starts a new journey parallel to Charles Darwin's writings called *Social Evolution.* The fourth chapter, entitled 'Emile Durkheim, 1858-1917', begins a further discussion in the sociology of how social order and consensus are to be reached which necessarily involves comparison with other groups. Chapter five, 'Max Weber, 1864-1920', deals with his effort to develop holistic sociology that he added to the issue of class identities, questions of status, political power, and analysis of various religions of the world.

I feel the book will be useful for most readers who want to learn about the theories of the founders of Sociology. I hope that readers find my effort worthwhile. I will thank all who favour me with their constructive suggestions for improving this volume.

SUJIT KUMAR CHOUDHARY

Acknowledgements

It gives me immense pleasure to express my gratitude to many who have directly or indirectly given a helping hand to complete this work. I am deeply indebted to all my teachers from the Centre for the Study of Social Systems, School of Social Sciences, Jawaharlal Nehru University (JNU), New Delhi, especially my Supervisors, Prof. Nandu Ram and Prof. K.L. Sharma. I am also grateful to Late Prof. Yogendra Singh, Prof. T.K. Oommen, Prof. Dipankar Gupta, Prof. Anand Kumar, Prof. Ehsanul Haq, Prof. Avijit Pathak, Prof. Susan Viswanathan, Prof. Maitrayee Chaudhuri, Prof. Nilika Mehrotra, Prof. Surinder Singh Jodhka, Prof. Vivek Kumar, and Prof. Amit Kumar Sharma for their constant intellectual support.

I want to acknowledge Dr B.R. Ambedkar Central Library, JNU, where I studied these founders' original works on sociology. My heartfelt gratitude also to Late Malik Sahab for his consistent and untiring support in finding the books in different libraries of JNU.

Coming to my family, I owe my heartfelt gratitude to my parents and all family members for their steadfast support and encouragement. My mother Namita Devi, wife Poly Choudhary, and son Akshit Kumar extended their help at various levels.

Last but not least, I must express my sincere thanks to all my colleagues and the intellectual fraternity of Sociology in India and the world over.

SUJIT KUMAR CHOUDHARY

CHAPTER 1

Auguste Comte 1798-1857

BIOGRAPHICAL SKETCH

Auguste Comte was a French philosopher who established a new discipline called *Sociology*. To him, the primary emphasis of sociology was on studying society scientifically. He had an enormous influence on early sociological theories, especially on the ideas of Herbert Spencer and Emile Durkheim. Isidore Auguste Marie François Xavier Comte, i.e. Auguste Comte was born in Montpellier in the southern part of France on 19 January 1798, in a Catholic Royalist family. His father was a government official in a lower position, but he wanted his son's career in politics. He joined the respected imperial lycée when he was only nine years old. At sixteen, he was admitted to one of France's most prestigious educational institutions, École Polytechnique. However, young Comte was sensitive to the social disorder of France resulting from the revolution. Due to this reason, he moved his attention toward human affairs and the study of society. École Polytechnique was known for its mathematical and natural sciences, that helped Comte's orientation of study about the liberation of humanity through a scientific development of human consciousness. As a result, Comte tried to find out some laws that could cure social ills such as crime, unemployment, wars, etc. At the same time, he became controversial at the École Polytechnique due to his explosive national politics and disputes over a policy issue. Due to this rebelliousness and strong decision-making on these issues, he left the school.

Auguste Comte (1798-1857)

Social philosophers such as L.G. Bonald and Joseph de Maistre influenced Comte at the École Polytechnique. Condorcet, a significant philosopher of France, believed that evolution occurs along with progress in human societies. Comte Henri de Saint-Simon (1760-1825), i.e. Saint-Simon had influenced Comte's intellectual thought. Comte later became a close friend and disciple of Saint-Simon.

Comte's central ambition was to reorganize human society based on political reformulation. According to him, such reorganization would depend upon humankind's spiritual and moral unification. Thus, Comte developed several central ideas in collaboration with Saint-Simon. Unfortunately, their partnership was short-lived and ended due to some problems.

Comte wrote his magnum opus *Cours de Philosophie Positive* between 1830 and 1842 and published it in 6 volumes. In this work, he developed the law of three stages and the conception of a science of society. At the age of forty and towards the end of this work, *Cours de Philosophie Positive*, Comte discovered the principle of 'cerebral hygiene'. Here, he began to practice 'cerebral hygiene' in which he stopped reading other peoples' work to keep his mind clear for his work.

From 1851 to 1854, he wrote a famous work entitled *System of Positive Politics* in 4 volumes. In these volumes, Comte applied theoretical sociology findings to solve his society's social problems. He met Clotilde de Vaux during this period, who became a very close friend. Unfortunately in 1846, Vaux died only a year after they met. Her death affected Comte greatly and his ideas turned towards mysticism and religion and devised a *Religion of Humanity*. He thought of himself as a priest. He has given to shape his thoughts on the *religion of humanity* in a written work entitled *Systeme de Politique Positive* (System of Positive Polity). After that, he started to work as a prophet of social regeneration and continued till his death on 5 September 1857, at the age of fifty-nine. However, his works were not recognized in France till his end. Comte's thinking could be seen in the French scientific movement of the last half of the nineteenth century, represented by Taine, Renan, Berthelot, and an outstanding English thinker John Stuart Mills.

I. THE LAW OF THREE STAGES

Auguste Comte has given the Law of Three Stages in his magnum opus *Course de Philosophie Positive* (The Course of Positivist Philosophy) which was written between 1830 and 1842. *Systeme de Politique Positive* (System of Positive Polity) was written between 1851 and 1854 and published in 1853, and 1912. In 1822, when he was working as Saint-Simon's Secretary, Comte attempted to discover the successive stages of the evolution of the human race. Thus, the Law of Human

Progress is also known as the Law of Three Stages. It is based on the method of scientific comparison of time.

Comte believed that the evolution of human society takes place with the growth of the human mind. Here, every branch of human knowledge passes through different stages of development, i.e., the theological, the metaphysical, and the scientific. The theory proposes these three intellectual stages that the world has passed throughout history. In this context, Comte stated:

> Each of our leading conceptions—'each branch of our knowledge, passes successively through different theoretical conditions: the Theological or fictitious; the metaphysical or abstract; and the scientific or positive. . . . In a theological state, the human mind, seeking the essential nature of beings, the first and final causes (the origin and purpose) of all effects . . . supposes all phenomena to be produced by the immediate action of supernatural beings. In the metaphysical state . . . the mind supposes . . . abstract forces, veritable entities (that is, personified abstractions) . . . capable of producing all phenomena. . . . In the final, the positive state, the mind has given over the vain search after Absolute notions, the origin and destination of the universe, and the causes of phenomena'. It applies itself to studying their laws—that is, their invariable relations of succession and resemblance. (Comte, 1912: 1-2)

In fact, in the first stage, man seeks a 'final cause', the second for 'abstract forces', and the third for 'exact laws'. Thus, the law of three stages of the evolution of human thought is discussed as follows:

1. *The Theological Stage*: According to Comte, this is the first stage of the evolution of human thought, and is also known as the fictitious stage. This stage characterized the world before 1300. During this period, the central idea was based on the belief in supernatural powers, religious figures, and gods and goddesses. Priests and the military-dominated this period. In particular, the social and physical world was seen as produced by God. 'The mind explains phenomena by

ascribing them to beings or forces comparable to the man himself' (Aron, 1965: 65-6). Thus, the human mind supposes that the immediate action of supernatural beings produces all phenomena. This stage has passed through three different phases—fetishism, polytheism, and monotheism.

Fetishism: Fetishism is composed of two words—'Fetish' means inanimate, and 'ism' means philosophy. This philosophy believes that supernatural power resides in an inanimate object with no priesthood. People believed in natural objects such as wood, stone, skull, etc. At the same time, they started believing in several gods in the form of natural things. Many fetishes created confusion for people, and finally, it gave the notion of polytheism.

Polytheism: 'Polytheism' is the belief in many gods. Human beings think that there would be a single god for a particular work. In this way, a variety of work that a person faces requires many gods. But the presence of many gods also created in people mental contradictions. So finally, they developed the idea of one God, i.e. monotheism.

Monotheism: 'Monotheism' believes in one God controlling and regulating everything.

In the theological stage, soldiers, kings, priests, etc., were given a leading position in society. In this stage, social organization was regulated by the military. It is the military power that provides the basis for social stability.

2. *The Metaphysical Stage:* According to Comte, this stage is the second stage in the evolution of human thought, and is also known as an abstract stage. This stage occurred roughly between 1300 and 1800. This stage of evolution involves understanding the belief that abstract forces such as 'nature' explain everything rather than supernatural beliefs. In this phase, 'the mind explains phenomena by invoking abstract entities like nature' (Aron, 1965: 66). Men started reasoning for themselves as per their understanding instead of accepting authoritative revelations in this stage. This stage was dominated by churchmen and lawyers.

3. *The Positive Stage*: This is the last and most scientific stage of the development of human thought. It is also known as the scientific stage. This stage finally entered in 1800. This stage is characterized by belief in science. It emphasizes the success of science and faith in positivism. It does not consider the idea of transcendentalism and supernaturalism. Coser explains 'human mind at this stage applies itself to studying their laws, i.e. their invariable relations of succession and resemblance' (Coser, 1996: 7). Human beings seek to establish laws that link facts and govern social life. Industrial administrators and scientists dominate this stage.

Comte believed that each stage or substage of human thought evolution necessarily grew from the preceding one. Thus, Comte argues, 'the constitution of the new system cannot take place before the destruction of the old' (Coser, 1912: 149). He also focused on three stages of development of human thought in correlation with the growth of a social organization, types of social order, types of social units, and material conditions found in society.

Comte identified two major types of societies based on three stages of human thought: the theological-military society and the scientific-industrial society. According to Comte, a particular 'type of society is dying, another born before his eyes. The dying type is characterized by. . . . Theological and military. . . . Theological thinking is contemporary with the predominance of military activity. . . . The type being born is scientific and industrial. This society is scientific in a sense . . . scientists are replacing priests or theologians as the social category providing the intellectual and moral foundation of the social order. The scientists are inheriting the spiritual power of the priests' (Aron, 1965: 64).

Comte analyses theological-military society's predominance of theological thinking and military activity. In the scientific-industrial society, theological ideas have been replaced by scientific ones that provide society's intellectual and moral foundation.

Comte's theory of human progress is considered a unilinear theory of evolution or social change. He believed that intellectual evolution is the essential basis of his explanation of human progress. He made a significant point that growth in the human population determines the rate of social progress. In this sense, Comte's approach to human progress seems to be holistic. The law of the three stages is linked with the hierarchy of the sciences.

II. HIERARCHY OF THE SCIENCES

Comte's second best-known theory, i.e. the hierarchy of the sciences, is related to the law of three stages. First, the hierarchy of the sciences is based on the notion that each subject has evolved from a general, simple to a highly complex level. In this regard, Comte says, 'Any kind of knowledge reaches the positive stage early in proportion to its generality, simplicity, and independence of other departments' (Comte, 1853: 6). Second, according to this view, a hierarchy of sciences represents the evolution of sciences from mathematics to sociology, i.e. mathematics, astronomy, physics, chemistry and biology. Finally, the discipline that is a positive science of society emerged in sociology. Hence, astronomy, the most general and straightforward of all-natural sciences, developed first, followed by physics, chemistry, biology, and sociology. 'Each science in this series depends for its emergence on the prior developments of its predecessors in a hierarchy marked by the law of increasing complexity and decreasing generality' (Coser, 1912: 9).

Comte's primary aim was to put forward his theory of the hierarchy of sciences to demonstrate the need for creating sociology and provide a foundation for the sociological concept of historical unity. Therefore, Comte began his analysis of the hierarchy of sciences by explaining two key concepts: analytic and synthetic. For Comte, 'the science of inorganic nature, physics and chemistry, is analytic because they establish laws among isolated phenomena' (Aron, 1965: 67). On the other hand, Biology is considered synthetic rather than analytic. It is because Biology explains an organ or a function of living creatures. 'It is within and about the whole organism that a particular biological act assumes its meaning and finds its explanation' (ibid.). The methodological approach of biological science prepares the foundation of social sciences, especially sociology.

The social sciences are considered more complex and dependent on their emergence on the development of all the other science disciplines. Due to this fact, the social sciences and especially sociology are the 'highest in the hierarchy'. Comte states: 'Social Science offers the attributes of completion of the positive method. All the others . . . are preparatory to it. Here alone can the general sense of natural law be decisively developed, by eliminating forever arbitrary wills and chimerical entities, in the most difficult case of all' (Comte, 1853: 383-4). Therefore, Social Science 'enjoys all the resources of the anterior sciences' (ibid.). But, so far as sociology is concerned, it is 'the gradual and continuous influence of generations upon each other' (ibid.: 261).

Sociology is different from its predecessors in the hierarchy. It is because of its specific methodology. But sociology stands nearer to and is dependent on biology. Sociology has various elements in common with biology, emphasizing organic or organismic unity. In addition biology cannot explain a function of an organ apart from the organism as a whole. Sociology cannot explain social phenomena without reference to the actual social context. Here, the idea of organic unity refers to the system's priority over an element that is taken as a whole rather than any particular element. Thus, Comte established a discipline of sociology based on a synthesis of the sciences. In this sense, sociology is the product of both objective and subjective synthesis of the sciences. Comte states: 'For there to be a synthesis, one must consider objectively the hierarchy of being ascending to the human species, and one must consider subjectively the knowledge that has a relation to man' (Aron, 1965: 106). Therefore, sociologists synthesize the findings of the sciences at both objective and subjective levels to achieve unity for humankind.

Another fact, according to Comte, is that sociology is the science of the human mind. 'Man understands the human mind only on condition that he observes its activity and its productions throughout history and in society' (Aron, 1965: 107). In a true sense, the science of the human mind is known as the sociology of knowledge. It is based on observation, analysis, and comprehension of the capacities of the human mind. The actual science of the human mind is developed through this production in the various stages of history. In this regard, 'The mind is social; it is historical: the mind of each age, the mind of each thinker, is caught in a social context' (ibid.).

Sociology, therefore, has emerged as the most complex science and arose much later than the other sciences. As a result, sociology studies more complex subjects than other sciences. Hence, the object of study of the different disciplines was relatively more straightforward than sociology. Comte accepted sociology as the 'crowing edifice' of the hierarchy of sciences in which he had in mind the general unifying nature of science. He was not claiming any superior status for sociology. On the contrary, he recognized a need to bring all sciences concerning each other with the help of positive knowledge.

In brief, the essential points of the hierarchy of the sciences can be outlined as follows:

(i) The hierarchical arrangement of the sciences is based on their historical emergence and development;
(ii) they are interdependent and interrelated to each other;
(iii) based on their decreasing order of generality and the increasing degree of complexity of their subject matter;
(iv) the growing degree of modification of the facts to study; and
(v) the ever-increasing nature of positive knowledge in terms of scientific methods from astronomy to sociology.

III. STATICS AND DYNAMICS SOCIOLOGY

Statics and Dynamics are the two basic categories of Auguste Comte's Sociology related to philosophy. This division comes from biology, which is the primary discipline of the hierarchy of sciences. The notion of social statistics and social dynamics deals with social progress and human development. These basic concepts discover those laws that make order and progress possible. In Volume II of the book *Positive Philosophy*, Comte wrote: 'The distinction is not between two classes of facts but between two aspects of a theory. It corresponds with the double conception of order and progress: for order consists . . . in a permanent harmony among the conditions of social existence, and progress consists in social development' (Comte, 1853: 218). Thus, it seems Statics and Dynamics, Progress and Order, are interrelated.

Statics studies the conditions of the existence of society, what Comte calls the social *consensus*. It is related to the social order. Social statics deals with the simple positive analysis of the anatomy of various societies and the bonds of mutual solidarity among the institutions of a particular collectivity. Comte writes about the foundations of social stability and social order in this context. According to him, 'The Statics study of sociology consists in the investigation of the laws of action and reaction of the different parts of the social system apart, for the occasion, from the fundamental movement which is always gradually modifying them' (ibid.: 219). Social statics studies the balance of mutual relations of elements within a social whole. There must be a 'spontaneous harmony between the whole and the parts of the social system' (ibid.: 222). Hence, social statics is a *theory of social order* which maintains harmony between the conditions of man's existence in society. Also social dynamics studies the continuous movement or laws of the succession of individual stages in society. In other words, 'Dynamics is the description of the successive stages through which human societies pass' (Aron, 1965: 90). Social dynamics is also known as the *theory of social progress*. According to him, Dynamics is a theory of social progress that amounts to society's fundamental development or evolution.

In addition, Comte's conception of statics is discussed in his major work *Systeme de Politique Positive* of Volume II. In this work, Comte divided the concept of statics into two parts: the study of human nature and social nature, and again the structure of human nature and the structure of social nature (Aron, 1965: 91).

Comte divides it into two or three parts in dealing with human nature. He considers a heart and a mind as constituent parts of the twofold divisions. If it is threefold, the heart divides into sentiment (or affection or emotion) and action (or will or courage). Man is emotional, active, and intelligent. According to Comte's famous formula, man is to act by emotion and *think to act.*

On the other hand, emotion will always be the soul of humanity and the soul of action. Intelligence will never be more than an organ to guide, direct, and control (ibid.: 92). Comte also suggested the breakdown of these three elements of human nature into various parts. First, the study of emotions is into two parts: egoism and altruism. Second, the study of intelligence is broken into two parts: understanding and expression. Understanding may be passive or active. Finally, the breakdown of the will is threefold: courage (to undertake), prudence (to execute), and steadfastness (to complete) (ibid.: 93-4).

Comte discusses the interpretation of social nature to deal with the second part of social statics. In this part, Comte outlined the theory of religion, theory of property, theory of the family, theory of language, and theory of the social organism or labour division.

Comte began his discussion by analysing the notion of religion in the social context. 'Religion is an inevitable part of every human society. Every society involves consensus, an agreement between groups, a contract between individuals, a unifying principle' (ibid.: 95). In this context, religion has played a significant role in uniting people. Religion is based on a unifying principle. In the words of Coser,

> Religion furnishes the unifying principle, the common ground without which individual differences would tear society apart. Religion permits men to overcome their egoistic propensities and to transcend themselves in the love of their fellow men. The powerful cement binds a society together in a common cult and belief system. Religion is at the root of social order. (1996: 11)

At the same time, religion also addresses the notion of intelligence, emotions, and the will of human nature simultaneously to create unity among individuals.

Property and language are the second and third dimensions of Comte's analysis of social nature. Property is the accumulation of goods transmitted from one generation to another, whereas language is the vessel in which it stores the thoughts of preceding generations. In this sense, property and language are the two essential human civilizing agents necessary to maintain the continuity of ideas of various generations. Coser explains it rightly, 'without common language men could never have attained solidarity and consensus; without this collective tool, no social order is possible' (ibid.: 11). Hence, a common language a medium of verbal interaction is indispensable for a human community.

Another crucial dimension of social nature is the family. The family is the primary social unit. Comte tried to understand the various relations existing within the family structure. These family relations are a relation of equality between brothers; a relation of veneration between children and parents; a complex relation of authority-obedience between husband and wife (Aron, 1965: 97). However, the family is the elementary social unit that fulfils the basic necessity of the individuals. As Comte says, 'It is by this avenue (of the family) that man comes forth from his mere personality and learns to live in another while obeying his most powerful instincts' (Comte, 1853: 281).

The division of labour is one of the essential and last part of Comte's analysis of social nature. Comte's division of labour is based on the differentiation of activities and man's co-operation. Division of labour links man and his fellows. Men are:

> Bound together by the very distribution of their occupations, this distribution causes the extent and growing complexity of the social organism. The social organization tends more and more to rest on an exact estimate of individual diversities, by so distributing employments as to appoint each one to the destination he is most fit for, from his own nature . . . from his education and his position, and, in short, from all his qualifications; so that all individual organizations, even the most vicious and imperfect . . . may finally be made use of for the general good (1853: 292).

Comte believed that the division of labour contributed to human solidarity by creating in each individual a sense of dependence on others. However, he also accepted that certain negative aspects of the division of labour are seen in modern industrial society. Comte finally expressed the hope that in the future, both temporal and spiritual powers would unite 'to keep up the idea of the whole and the feeling of the common interconnection' (ibid.: 294).

Comte's analysis of social nature is regarded as functional. His analysis of social institutions, whether language or religion or the division of labour or family, emphasizes the inter-connectedness of all these phenomena that maintain broader social order. In this context, Comte says,

> There must always be a spontaneous harmony between the parts and the whole of the social systems. . . . It is evident that not only must political institutions and social manners, on the one hand, and manners and ideas on the other, be always mutually connected; but further than this consolidated whole must always be connected, by its nature, with the corresponding state of the integral development of humanity. (1853: 222)

In brief, social statics and social dynamics are simply the study of coexistence on the one hand and succession on the other. These are the study of the essential human and social order, of its transformations and fulfilment. Scientific terms—Statics and Dynamics represent philosophical terms—order and progress, respectively. Despite the difference between Statics and Dynamics, they are linked together throughout the system.

IV. METHODOLOGY

Auguste Comte is accepted as the founding father of sociology who had initially used the term *social physics* for the study of society. However, he was convinced that a Belgian Scientist, Adolphe Quetelet, used the same term to describe simple statics and hence he finally changed it into Sociology. Comte's methodology is related to the methods of the natural sciences. According to him, societies should be studied using the same techniques as in the natural sciences, known as *positivism*. The society of human beings, argues Comte, must be studied in the same scientific manner as the world of nature. Natural sciences' progress in establishing laws such as Newton's law of gravity and Copernicus's law of planet led him to believe that we can discover social rules even in society.

According to *positivism*, 'If sociology is to study and acquire knowledge of social life, it must be a science and must follow the standard method of the sciences' (Cuff et al., 1990: 195). Sociology, hence, must use 'positivist' methods to discover social law. 'The idea of treating social science', Comte explained in the *system of positive polity*, 'as an application of mathematics to give it a positive character had its source in the metaphysical prejudice that outside of mathematics there can be no real certainty' (1853: 52). Therefore, Auguste Comte was considered at the forefront of the development of *positivistic sociology*.

Comte's science of society, i.e. sociology, is equated with the approaches and methods of natural sciences. 'Positivism consists of observing phenomena, analysing them, and discovering the laws governing the relations among them' (Aron, 1965: 85). In the positivistic study of sociology, Comte used three methods of inquiry that have been used in the natural sciences: *observation*, *experimentation*, and *comparison*. These scientific methods, i.e. observation, experimentation, and comparison, must be used in combination with *the historical method*. 'The historical comparison of the consecutive states of humanity is not only the chief scientific device of the new political philosophy . . . it constitutes the substratum of the science, in whatever is essential to it' (Comte, 1853: 251). The historical method is used to search the general laws of the successive transformations of humanity through fixed stages of historical periods.

Observation is the first method of inquiry in Comte's methodology of sciences. Observation involved the guidance of a preparatory theory. 'No social fact can have any scientific meaning till it is connected with some other social fact' (1853: 245) by a preliminary theory. Hence, observation can come into its own only when it is subordinated to phenomena statics and dynamic law (ibid.). This scientific method of investigation applies to all social sciences disciplines in general and sociology in particular. The second scientific method of inquiry, experimentation, is partly applicable to the social sciences. Direct experimentation is not feasible in the human world. But 'experimentation *takes place whenever the regular course of the phenomenon is interfered* with in any determinate manner . . . Pathological cases are the true scientific equivalent of pure experimentation' (ibid.: 246). *Experimentation* in sociology, according to Comte, means *controlled observation*, in which the scrutiny of 'pathological cases' gives privileged access to an understanding of the normal. The third scientific method of investigation, *Comparison*, has got central importance for sociologists. The comparison involved between human and animal, society and society, like and unlike, etc. Sociology is, says Comte,

> a comparison of the different coexisting states of human society on the various parts of the earth's surface, these states being completely independent of each other. By this method, the different stages of evolution may all be observed at once. (1853: 249)

In this context, the notion of the comparative method is essential to study various types of societies. Hence, historical comparisons throughout humanity's evolution are at the core of sociological inquiry.

In conclusion, Comte's sociological method assured the scientific quality of 'social physics' that involved observation, experimentation, and comparison and the historical method. Comte argued the utility and usefulness of these natural methods in sociology as follows: 'We shall find that there is no chance of order and agreement but in subjecting social phenomena, like all others, to invariable natural laws, which shall, as a whole, prescribe for each period, with entire certainty, the limits, and character of social action' (Comte, 1853: 14).

V. SCIENTIFIC THEORY OF MORALITY AND RELIGION OF HUMANITY

The notion of morality and the religion of humanity are central to Comte's philosophical and sociological thought. Comte had conceived the religion of humanity only when he had been in love with Clotilde de Vaux. Comte understood the importance of human unity and considered sociology the religion of human unity. Comte wanted men to be united by common convictions and a single object of their love. He believed in creating a new social order based on moral unity and new religion of humanity. Therefore, Comte thought of himself as the founder of the religion of humanity. He tried to understand and discuss religion and morality based on scientific principles, i.e. *positivism*.

Comte's religion reveals itself more clearly in his principle of humanism. He defines the religion of humanity as 'the state of complete harmony peculiar to human life, in its collection as well as its individual form when all the parts of life are ordered in their natural relations to each other' (Ellwood, 1955: 402). Comte's supreme reality is that all other human facts are subject and humanity's ultimate reality. Humanity, thus, becomes the centre of worship of all positivistic scientists.

Humanity has two dimensions: first, humanity may be regarded as an object of investigation and study for science. Second, humanity may also be considered an object of love, adoration and social service (Ellwood, 1955: 403-4). Hence, Comte's humanity becomes a central stage of religion and morality.

To Comte, according to traditional conception, man can no longer believe in revelation, the church's catechism, or divinity. Man needs religion because he needs spiritual power based on love (Aron, 1965: 107). In this context, Comte's sociocracy seems to be philosophically relevant here. According to sociocracy,

> The new positive society will be an organic, hierarchic based on the natural talents of Individuals . . . The goal of every individual will be to rise in the spiritual hierarchy of merit and moral worth, not the temporal hierarchy of wealth and power . . . the only hierarchy that counts in the positive sociocracy is the hierarchy of merit and heat. The new society of peace and harmony will endure if it is tempered and regulated by moral and spiritual power. (Abraham & Morgan, 1985: 17-18)

Therefore, the hierarchy of moral worth must be created, which is opposed to the temporal order.

In the religion of humanity, Comte had great hope for the reorganization of society. At this point, sociologists have a greater responsibility in constructing the future of humankind. For this, the sociologist must attempt to form a group of secular priests who would work on the new positive religion's spiritual power. These secular priests would act as the moral guides of the community and regulate the process of education. 'Live for others' will be the supreme command of the religion of humanity. This new positivist order of humankind would have 'Love' as its primary principle, order as its basis, and progress as its aim.

VI. CONCLUSION

Auguste Comte has made a significant contribution to the development of new science of society called *Sociology*. The steps involved in the emergence of Comte's sociology were from *social physics* to the reorganization of society. Comte is considered an evolutionary sociologist for his contribution to the law of three stages and the hierarchy of sciences. However, Comte's law of three stages has been more or less rejected by contemporary sociologists. But the essential stages of development in ideas and culture in a modified form have been accepted. In establishing the hierarchy of the sciences, Comte takes the methodological orientation of the various disciplines. In the last stage of the hierarchy of sciences, he accepted the emergence of sociology as the most complex, scientific, and synthetic discipline of science. Society would be studied more scientifically by the method of natural sciences called *positivism*. *Positivism* is his methodological tool for studying society in which observation, comparison, experimentation, and historical methods are involved.

In the latter period of his life, Comte's thoughts took a new direction, from the positivistic orientation of society to establishing a humanitarian understanding of society. Comte's humanitarian, therefore, was reflected in his description of the function of the new science, i.e. Sociology. Social Science, argues Comte, must ultimately be dedicated to the concrete benefit of humankind—to facilitate the human condition. Thus, his main interest was to establish the discipline of sociology, which is the study of the social background of human history systematically into one body of knowledge and prepare a practical approach to social reform based on a lasting order of principles of humanity and morality. At this juncture, Comte emphasized that the sociologist must understand three components of society—a common language, religion, and division of labour within society. Moreover, these three components have a significant role in the evolution of society from one stage to the other. Comte describes the functional relation between Statics (order) and Dynamics (progress) in this context.

Comte's ideas anticipate most trends that are observable in contemporary sociology. Thus, the significant contributions of Comte provide a vast horizon for the coming sociologists in the field of sociological methods, sociological approaches and perspectives, sociological concepts and theories on the one hand, and philosophy of society on the other.

KEY TERMS

Dynamics: It is any mass, object, or force in a state of motion. In society, it describes the notion of social change.

Evolution: The process of slow changes through a long time in which life forms have developed from simple unicellular beings, such as amoeba, to complex multicellular beings, like human beings.

Experiment: A scientific method of investigation used by Comte. An experiment involves the investigator's intervention to observe the investigation phenomena under controlled conditions.

Heuristic Assumption: An assumption made not because it has been established that it is true but because it is considered helpful in an investigation. The heuristic assumption is regarded as a utilitarian device intended to aid in discovering new facts and relationships.

Hierarchy: A relationship of individuals, groups or classes involving a ranking system. Comte has used hierarchy concerning the hierarchy of disciplines of sciences.

Historical Method: The historical method evaluates sources of information about the past to determine their reality. It also involves the analysis of authentic sources for detailed data about the period being studied.

Human Nature: Those behavioural characteristics common to men everywhere, in all societies, past and present. The concept of human nature focuses on the individual personality. But, in essence, it deals with the universal human qualities that everywhere result from the impact of the requirements of social life on the human organism. Comte used it in the analysis of social statics.

Induction: The logical process in which generalizations are inferred from specific facts. The experimental method is inductive, where conclusions are derived from individual observations.

Language: A universal form of human behaviour involving symbolic communication through a culturally accepted system of a sound pattern having standardized meaning. Language is a social product. Comte used this term in the analysis of the social nature of statics.

Love: Strong emotional identification with another, which is the basis of a gratifying or potentially gratifying social relationship. Love is an essential part of Comte's analysis of the humanity of religion.

Metaphysical: Comte has used it to denote a stage of development of the mind in which the reason explains the phenomenon by invoking abstract entities or forces like 'nature'. In this stage, human beings explain the meaning of this word in terms of 'essence', 'ideas', etc. It is one of the second stages of Comte's law of three stages.

Methodology: The logic of scientific investigation is called methodology. In this sense, methodology in sociology includes the analysis of the basic assumption of science in general and sociology in particular. In addition, in theory, construction, the interrelationship of theory and research, and the procedures of empirical investigation are involved.

Objectivity: In scientific research, the quality is expressed to eliminate biases in thought and empirical processes to achieve the most unbiased and universal generalizations possible under the conditions of knowledge.

Observation: It is the examination of behaviour directly by an investigator or persons who serve as observers. Comte used it in his methodology as one of the essential methods of inquiry of scientific investigation.

Positive: Positive is one of the last and most important stages of Comte's law of the three stages of the development of human thought. Human beings search for social laws that link facts and govern social life in the positive stage.

Positivism: The philosophical position holds that knowledge can be derived only from sensory experience. Auguste Comte is regarded as the founder of positivism. Positivism is mainly based on the methods used in the natural sciences.

Science: Systematized knowledge derived from observation, experimentation, and comparison is science. Thus, scientific knowledge can be tested, verified, or proved.

Scientific Method: Building a body of scientific knowledge through observation, experimentation, generalization and verification is called the scientific method. The scientific method depends on the collection of empirical facts. Therefore, theory construction is a vital part of scientific methods.

Social Dynamics: Auguste Comte referred to the study of society in terms of interrelated social processes and the successive stages of social change.

Social Physics: Auguste Comte used the term for the new science of society, which he later (1838) replaced with the term *Sociology*.

Social Reorganization: The process of cooperative action to counteract undesirable conditions in society. Comte used this term in the analysis of the humanity of religion.

Social Statics: Auguste Comte used the term to refer to the study of *social structure* and the interrelations of its various parts. The examination of *social statics*, according to Comte, consists of human and social nature.

Theological: The literal meaning of theology is the study of religion. It is the first stage of the development of human thought. At this stage, the notion of spirits and supernatural beings played a significant role.

REFERENCES

Abraham, Francis and John Henry Morgan, *Sociological Thought from Comte to Sorokin*, Macmillan India Limited, Madras, 1985.

Aron, Raymond, *Main Currents in Sociological Thought*, vol. I, Penguin Books, USA, 1965, pp. 65-6.

Comte, Auguste, *Course de Philosophie Positive* (The Course of Positivist Philosophy or the Positive Philosophy), translated and condensed by Harriet Martineau, Trubner, London, 1853.

——, *System de Politique Positive* (System of Positive Polity or Positive Polity), Four Volumes, IV, Cres, Paris, 1912.

Coser, Lewis A., *Masters of Sociological Thought*, Rawat Publications, Jaipur, 1996.

Cuff, E.C., W.W. Sharrock and D.W. Francis, *Perspectives in Sociology*, Third Edition, Unwin Hyman, London, 1990.

CHAPTER 2

Karl Heinrich Marx 1818-1883

BIOGRAPHICAL SKETCH

Karl Marx (Rubel & Manale, 1975) was born in Trier, a small city in the German Rhineland, on 5 May 1818. He belonged to a middle-class Jewish family but was converted to Protestant Christianity to escape the social difficulty of Jews in German society. Marx's father, a lawyer, played a significant role in acting as his advisor and friend. In 1835, Marx entered the University of Bonn as a law student and was transferred to the University of Berlin in 1836. In 1841, Marx was awarded a PhD degree from the University of Berlin. It was a university influenced by Hegel and Young Hegelians.

Karl Marx was invited by a Cologne publicist, Moses Hess, to write articles for a journal, *Rheinische Zeitung*. Later, he became its chief editor. Marx's work was shaped by his criticism of Hegel and Hegel's dominance in German philosophy. In 1843, Marx produced two major writings criticizing Hegel's conception of the state, *A Critique of Hegel's Philosophy of Right* and *On the Jewish Question* (Marx, 1870; Tucker, 1978). After making these critiques, he developed an outline of a theory of History and economic aspects—an idea which later became one of Marx's most important contributions.

Marx married in 1843, and he left Germany to get the liberal atmosphere in Paris. In France, he continued to grapple with the ideas of Hegel and the Young Hegelians, but he also encountered two new sets of ideas—French socialism and English political economy (Ritzer, 1988: 40). In addition, he developed the idea of political economy by reading the works

Karl Heinrich Marx (1818-1883)

of Adam Smith and David Ricardo. Finally, Marx combined Hegelianism, socialism and political economy which shaped his intellectual orientation. At the same time, he met Friedrich Engels, who became his lifelong friend, benefactor, and collaborator. Marx came to know from Engels about misery as a working-class man. Marx drafted some facts related to classical economics and alienated labour entitled the *Economic and Philosophic Manuscripts,* one of his most significant works by May of 1844. Marx emphasized the formal study of political economy and economic questions in this work.

The Prussian government was upset by some of his writings. As a result, the French government expelled Marx in 1845 at the request of Prussian government. Marx then migrated to Brussels, where his work grew with Engels. One of the first writings of their collaboration was *The Holy Family,* which attacked the Young Hegelians for their conservative view of society and state (Marx & Engels, 1956). Later, Marx and Engels wrote a manuscript entitled *The German Ideology*, which laid out the conditions of the break with German philosophy and outlined the overview of the materialistic theory of History (Marx & Engels, 1947).

In Brussels, Marx's radicalism continued to grow, and he became an active member of the famous international revolutionary movement. He was also associated with the Communist League and was asked to write a document (with Engels) expounding its aims and beliefs. The result was the publication of *The Communist Manifesto* of 1848, a work that was characterized by ringing political slogans. This work had an enormous impact on the workers movement throughout Europe. In 1849, Marx moved to London. In light of his failure in the political revolutions of 1848, he began to withdraw from active revolutionary activity and started severe and detailed research on the capitalist system. By 1859, he published *A Contribution to the Critique of Political Economy*, the famous preface of one of the most frequently quoted excerpts from his writings (Marx, 1977). Later, Marx published the first volume of *Capital*, his magnum opus, in 1867. The second and third volumes were edited after Marx's death by Engels. Again, Capital created a stir, translated into French, English, Russian, and Italian. Lastly, after a prolonged illness in the lungs, he died in his sleep on 14 March 1883, in London at the age of 65.

I. HEGELIAN AND MARXIAN THOUGHT

Neither any idea nor intellectual understanding of Marx's work is possible without considering George Hegel's work. Hegel made a significant contribution to developing Marx's philosophical and dialectical thought. Hegel was a dominant philosopher and was the originator of one of the essential philosophical doctrines of the nineteenth century, called philosophical idealism. Collins explains it,

Hegel's philosophy culminated in the idealist tradition that began with Kant; it held that the essence of reality is the reason. The spirit of Reason manifests itself only gradually, revealing more and more facets of itself over time. (1972: 34)

According to the idealist tradition, reason is the essence of reality, and reason expresses itself during history. This tradition starts with Immanuel Kant and reaches its peak with Hegel.

Idealism is defined as a philosophical perspective concerned with the ultimate conditions of human existence. Its development can be arrived at only by examining abstract philosophic categories. From a philosophical perspective, idealism claimed that the fundamental task of philosophy and social thought was to understand human existence by looking at conceptual categories such as being, reason, history and spirit. The importance of Hegel's observation was that it viewed the world, reality and being in terms of interrelated processes rather than seeing individuals and history as separate, free-standing entities. Hegel denotes the interconnectedness between the human and historical realms: spirit, reason, being, and history (Morrison, 1995: 29). Hegel assumes that the abstract categories of 'history', 'spirit' and 'reason' are the ultimate subject matter of philosophical investigation. Mark's rejection of Hegel's philosophical viewpoint was central to his thinking and discussed in his early work—*The Holy Family*.

Marx wanted to develop an understanding of reality and history. Therefore, Marx outlined the conditions to reject Hegel's philosophical idealism based on four central theoretical premises. First, he objected to the fundamental task of philosophy that examined the role played by the abstract categories of history and spirit in human development. Second, he argued that Hegel's idealist view led to a fundamental misunderstanding of human existence because it concluded that only philosophic categories are real (Rotenstreich, 1965). Third, he took the idea that idealist philosophers put forward which referred neither to concrete human activity nor physical reality, but only to be grasped as ideas. Finally, Marx believed that when the existence of human beings is understood only as 'ideas and thought', the more real and practical problems of individual lives are overlooked (Morrison, 1995: 30).

Another point of Marx's disagreement with Hegel was over the role of ideas in history (Colletti, 1979). Hegel stressed the centrality of reason in human history and placed theoretical emphasis on the 'ideal' category. He believed that human reason is the highest good. Contrary to that, Marx thought individuals have physical needs and requirements that sustain their lives. Therefore, Marx accepted the idea of materialism in opposition to idealism.

Marx also disagreed with Hegel's view regarding the ultimate role of society and the state. Hegel's philosophical perspective took a conservative picture of history and society. Hegel thought that society and the state had developed out of what he called the forces of the spirit in history and the actualization of ethics (Hegel, 1958: 218). In this way, Hegel supported the state with a kind of 'eternal' quality in its activities that were unalterable. Marx rejected this view by stating that Hegel had created the illusion that inequality and human hardship were natural outcomes of history rather than resulting from society's natural disadvantages and historical social inequalities (Morrison, 1995: 31).

Marx's last point of disagreement with Hegel's understanding was human hardship and social inequality.

> Hegel had claimed that hardship and suffering stem from a kind of consciousness existing in the minds of individuals rather than in the form of material obstacles which exist in reality and hinder individual freedom. For Marx, the answer to social inequality and human hardship lay not in abstract forces of the development of consciousness but rather in the concrete material conditions that make it necessary for one class of persons to dominate others. (Morrison, 1995: 31-2)

MATERIALISM—A NEW THEORETICAL INTERPRETATION

Marx's criticism of idealism finally laid down a new theoretical framework to understand society and history from the materialist perspective. Marx was interested in analysing nature and meaning and the truth of history based on 'materialistic' interpretation rather than Hegelian idealism.

Materialism is a theoretical perspective that looks at human problems by studying the actual conditions of human existence. The basis of materialism is to satisfy their material needs, i.e. food, shelter and clothing. Thus, materialism is a theoretical perspective in which human beings must fulfil their everyday economic needs through physical labour and practical, productive activity (Marx & Engels, 1947: 16). Hence, materialism has taken the most basic human act as its starting point—economic production.

II. HISTORICAL MATERIALISM: THE MATERIALIST THEORY OF HISTORY

The materialist theory of history is one of Marx's significant social and political thinking, and it remains one of his most central and influential works. Marx developed the materialist theory of history in his major work, *The German Ideology* with Engels. *The German Ideology* was written between 1845 and 1846 and published in 1846. The aim to establish this theory was to set out the views of materialism as opposite to Hegelian philosophy.

Marx outlined some of the primary issues before discussing historical materialism in terms of propositions related to understanding historical and social processes from the perspective of human economic activity. First, Marx believed that, before anything else, human beings must be able to obtain food, shelter, and clothing to live (Marx & Engels, 1947: 7-9). Thus, the first and most important historical act is producing the means to satisfy human economic needs. Marx states:

> The first premise of all human existence, and therefore of all history, is that human beings must be in a position to live to be able to 'make history'. But, life involved before eating, drinking, habitation, clothing and many other things. The first act is thus the production of

the means to satisfy these needs, the production of material life itself. (ibid.)

Second, human beings distinguish themselves from animals to the extent that they produce the standards to meet their primary material needs (Marx & Engels, 1947: 7). Third, how humans produce depends on what they find in nature and what they must produce to survive (ibid.).

Historical materialism is one of the critical theories of Marx's sociological understanding. According to Engels, the theory of historical materialism was discovered by Karl Marx, but Marx thought Friedrich Engels independently conceived the materialist formulation of history. Marx discussed his theory of historical materialism in 'Preface' to *A Contribution to the Critique of Political Economy* (1859). It is one of the most intelligent summaries of this theory as written by Marx:

> In the social production which men carry on they enter into definite relations that are indispensable and independent of their will. These relations of production correspond to a definite stage of the development of their material forces of production. The totality of these relations of production constitutes the economic structure of society, which is the fundamental foundation on top of which arises a legal and political superstructure to which correspond definite forms of social consciousness. It is not the consciousness of men that determines their existence, but instead, their social existence determines their consciousness. At a particular stage of their development, the material forces of production in society come in conflict with the existing relations of production, or—what is but a legal expression of the same thing—with the property relations within which they had been at work before. From forms of development of the forces of production, these relations turn into their fetters. Then occurs a period of social revolution. With the change of the economic foundation, the entire immense superstructure is more or less rapidly transformed. (Marx, 1859: 20-1)

Here, he says that the fundamental basis of society is its economic structure. From this central theme, we find that there are four basic concepts to the materialist theory of history: (i) means of production; (ii) relations of production; (iii) modes of production; and (iv) forces of production. To see the wholistic interpretation of this theory, we begin to look at the concept of means of production.

MEANS OF PRODUCTION

According to Marx, the means of production refers to anything in the external world used to produce essential material needs and maintain existence. Thus, land, animals, tools, machinery, etc., are considered the means of production. However, the fact is that these production conditions are occupied by a particular class of people, leading to the division of society into different economic classes (Marx, 1846: 8-13). The primary division, according to Marx, is between two classes, owners and non-owners, of the means of production. These classes denote that one class owns the means of production while the other is subject to those who rule over them (Marx, 1846: 9). The non-owners class is the direct producer of material goods, but they cannot satisfy their material needs without the owners' permission.

RELATIONS OF PRODUCTION

Relations of production are the second fundamental concept of the materialist theory of history. The importance of relations of production lies in the fact that it economically binds one class to another. Relations of production refer to social relationships that arise directly out of the process of production. These relationships include the relationships between the owners and non-owners of the means of production. These relationships decide and even determine the control and the capacity to possess the product.

The central theme of relations of production is that non-owners are compelled to enter into production relations to satisfy their own economic needs. As a result, the non-owners are subordinated to the class who are dominant over them. It gives rise to several key consequences of the relations of production outlined by Cohen (Cohen, 1978). First, non-owners produce for other's use rather than for themselves; second, the livelihoods of the non-owners depend on their relations with their owners; third, the dominant classes have direct rights over the economic product of the producer; fourth, the owners of the means of production always receive more from the production process than the producer and fifth, non-owners are subject to the authority of their superiors (Cohen, 1978: 69-70).

Relations of production appear in different stages of the economic development of every type of society. For instance, patricians and slaves in ancient societies were based on a system of production in which a class of military rulers enslaved populations who produced directly for those who ruled over them. Lord and Serf, on the other hand, in feudal society, where economic production was based on an aristocratic class of landholders who relied on an inserted peasantry to perform necessary labour. Finally, capitalist and wage labourers in capitalist societies are based on a large class of wage labourers who produce surplus value (profit) for the class that rules them (Morrison, 1995: 38).

MODES OF PRODUCTION

Modes of production is the fourth and most important concept of the materialist theory of history. A mode of production is defined as the relationship between the relations of production and the forces of production. The different relationships can distinguish modes of production between the forces and relations of production (Cornforth, 1962: 36).

In addition, the mode of production is its ability to determine the system of social relations arising from it, i.e. each mode of production has its specific relation to production. For instance, the primary way of producing economic necessities in feudal society is cultivation. It produces food crops, domestic animals, shelter and clothing. In this way, the production process leads to forming of a system of social relations in terms of lord and serf. Morrison concluded by stating: 'The mode of production allowed Marx to identify the primary economic elements of a historical period by showing how its economic base directly shaped its system of social relations' (1995: 40).

Marx believed that the division of society into owners and non-owners of the means of production is a law of historical development. To explain, he divided history into four stages of development: Asiatic, ancient, feudal and capitalist. These historical stages of development were based on the mode of production (Marx & Engels, 1846: 9-13).

(i) *Asiatic or Tribal Mode of Production:* Asiatic mode of production refers to a community-based production system where land ownership is *communal. Its existence is expressed through the real or imaginary unity* of these communities. Therefore, this mode of production is the characteristic of a primitive community in which land ownership is communal. These communities are mainly based on kinship relations. The division of labour is rudimentary, there is no development of private property, and the social structure is derived from the family and kinship group. It is a type of classless society.

(ii) *Ancient Mode of Production:* The ancient mode of production was the second mode of production. This form of social organization develops from an association of tribes that form an organization of city-states. The productive system is mainly agrarian with a rudimentary industry and a system of trade and commerce (Marx & Engels, 1846: 9). Slavery was part of the ancient mode of production. In contrast to tribal society, there is private property and class relations develop from property ownership. Thus, masters and slaves were two social classes found in ancient society. In this production system, the master had the right of ownership over the slave and the slaves' labour products.

This type of society occupies vast territories. In an ancient mode of production, the productive system has an extensive division of labour and a civil, political and military authority evolves as an adjunct to the productive system. The ancient

Greco-Roman world is a historical example of productive systems where labour was in the form of slavery (ibid.).

(iii) *Feudal Mode of Production:* The third form of mode of production ownership is a feudal society. This production system is agriculture-based, and the powerful means of producing food is based on the land. The focal point of production is agriculture developed in the countryside or village. There is no development of industry and town life (Marx & Engels, 1846: 11-13). The feudal mode of production is concerned with two classes, the feudal lords and the serfs. The feudal lords had property rights, whereas the serfs were deprived. In this condition, serfs were obliged to surrender their labour to fulfil familial requirements. In other words, the feudal lords exploited their tenants or 'serfs'. Hence, the feudal mode of production refers to a production system where the lords take advantage of surplus labour from the serfs in the form of rent.

Feudal society was seen by Marx and Engels as intermediate, i.e. between the slave society and the capitalist society. The evolution of the feudal system brought about the exchange of agricultural and manufactured products in regional markets. Between the ninth and the seventeenth centuries, feudal societies were dominant throughout Europe and England.

(iv) *Capitalist Mode of Production:* The fourth form of mode of production was the capitalist mode of production. The capitalist mode of production evolved from the destruction of a feudal mode of production and a transformation of production from the countryside to the town. The class of serfs of feudal society was replaced by the wage labourers of capitalist society. The productive system is based on an advanced division of labour, with developed trade and commercial activity. In a capitalist mode of production, the town has become the centre of economic activity. The productive system has shifted from agriculture to industry, where there is a fully developed political and civil life. There is widespread emergence of private property and an expanded class system of capitalists, who are the owners of the means of production. On the other hand, there are other classes of wage labourers who are producers of physical labour (Marx & Engels, 1846: 43-78).

The capitalist mode of production refers to a production system where the owners of the means of production are the capitalists, who capture surplus labour from the proletariats in the form of profits. Capitalism refers to a mode of production in which capital is the dominant means of production. In the beginning, capitalism emerged in Europe and then in other parts of the world. The industrial revolution started in England and spread across different countries, which saw a rapid growth of technology and the corresponding rise of a capitalist economy. Marx viewed capitalism as a historical phase, eventually replaced by socialism—a revolutionary change from capitalism to socialism. As Marx stated,

> at a certain stage of development, the material forces of production in society come in conflict with the existing relations of production, or—what is but a legal expression of the same thing—with the property relations within which they had been at work before. From forms of development of the forces of production, these relations turn into their fetters. Then occurs a period of social revolution. With the change of the economic foundation the entire immense superstructure is more or less rapidly transformed. (Marx, 1977: 20-1)

For Marx, each of these stages of historical development has three central themes: (i) they perpetuate the division of society into classes, namely two classes, where one class is dominant over another; (ii) they perpetuate economic, political and social inequality; and (iii) in each society, unequal social relations are supported by religion, law, and the political structure.

FORCES OF PRODUCTION

Forces of production are the third fundamental concept of the materialist theory of history. Forces of production refer to the material-technical aspect of production and the corresponding labour power and its competencies required in the production process. In a nutshell, the forces of production, according to Marx, include means of production and labour-power. The development of machinery, changes in the labour process, and the opening up of the workers are included in the forces of production.

The 'Forces' and 'Relations' of production are interlinked and interrelated. The development of one leads to a growing incompatibility or contradiction with the other. The contradiction between the two aspects of production is 'act as the motor of History' (Bottomore, 1975: 178).

III. INTERPRETATION OF IDEOLOGY

Marx developed his general theory of Ideology with Engels between 1845 and 1846. The theory of ideology follows directly from the materialist theory of history and has been discussed in the first section of *The German Ideology*, entitled, 'Feuerbach' (Marx & Engels, 1975: 35-7, 59-62). An ideology can be defined as an integrated system of external and coercive ideas of people (Lefebvre, 1968). The central theme of the theory of ideology, according to Marx, is: 'It is not the unfolding of ideas that explains the historical development of society (as Hegel and Comte would have argued), but the development of the social structure in response to changing material conditions that explain the emergence of new ideas' (Johnson, 1981: 132). According to Marx, ideas belong to the realm of the superstructure and are determined by the economic infrastructure. Thus ideas, according to Marx, are historical outcomes of economic activity. To understand the theory of ideology, Morrison (1995: 44) categorized it into four building blocks of ideology: (i) the relationship between ideas and material activity in society; (ii) the relationship between the concept of ideology and a theory of perception; (iii) the relationship between ideology and the dominant class; and (iv) the functions of ideology.

The first building block of a theory of ideology is the link between ideas and the material base of society. Marx thought that ideas have their origin in the material base of society and that 'the production of ideas is directly interwoven with material activity' (Marx & Engels, 1947). The simple fact is that the first act of individuals is always economic because human beings must produce to live. Two important conclusions can be drawn in this regard: (i) the act of economic production shapes social relations and, therefore, the structure of society; and (ii) economic production gives rise to a system of ideas and beliefs which come to represent the productive relative relations that stand as 'conscious images in mental life' (Marx & Engels, 1947: 14-16). Therefore, it can be said that ideas are linked with the material activity of society.

The second building block of a theory of ideology is concerned with the concept of ideology and its relationship with the individual's internal perception of the outer world. In this context, Marx has defined the concept of ideology in two ways. The first states: 'if in all ideology human beings and their relations appear upside down as in a camera obscura, this phenomenon arises just as much from their historical life processes as the inversion of objects on the retina does from their physical life processes' (Marx & Engels, 1947: 14). The second definition states: 'if in their imagination (individuals) turn reality upside down, then this, in turn, results from their limited material mode of activity and their limited social relations arising from it' (Marx & Engels, 1947: 36). From these two quotations, we can outline the following points regarding ideology.

First and foremost, ideology is a system of attitudes, conceptions, ideas, and beliefs capable of (i) making circumstances appear 'upside down'; and (ii) 'inverting' our perception of reality. These two essential ideology features are most important since they alter our perception of the outer world or objective social reality (Morrison, 1995: 45-6). For Marx, society is always thought of as a historical product of human actors. In this sense, individuals are actively related to history through their material activity. Therefore, consciousness, according to Marx, must be a social product. In this context, it is necessary to cite Marx's famous phrase 'Social existence determines consciousness'. Hence, the central methodological premise here is that individual perception of reality is tied to material conditions and consciousness.

The third building block of the theory of ideology is the relationship between ideology and the interests of the dominant class. Marx believed that the ideologies prevailing at any particular time reflect the worldview of the dominant class. In other words, ideas depend on social positions, particularly on the class positions of their proponents. Marx wrote:

> The idea of the ruling class is in every epoch the ruling ideas, i.e. the class, which is the ruling material force of society, is at the same time its ruling intellectual force. The class which has the means of material production at its disposal has control at the same time over the means of mental production, so that thereby generally speaking, the ideas of those who lack the means of mental production are subject to it. The ruling ideas are nothing more than the ideal expression of the dominant material relationships, the dominant material relationships grasped as ideas; hence of the relationship which makes the one class the ruling one, therefore the *ideas* of its dominance. (Marx & Engels, 1947: 39)

Marx refers to the dominant ideas of each epoch as 'ruling class ideology'. From the above quotation, we find: first, the class which presides over the means of material production 'control the means of mental production' (Marx & Engels, 1947: 39). Second, the dominant classes represent their interests as the common interest. This interest takes on the character of an 'ideal form' and 'represents them as the only universally valid ideas' (Marx & Engels, 1947: 40-1). Ideas and beliefs represent only the will and interests of a dominant class. In realizing the interests of only one class, these social relations stand in contradiction to the class of workers. In this sense, ideology legitimates and justifies the reality of one class.

The fourth building block of a theory of ideology concerns the functions of ideological arrangements in society. Ideology has several explicit functions: first, ideology conceals social contradictions from class distinctions. Second, ideology resolves the inconsistencies favouring the dominant classes and their interests. Third, ideology legitimizes the system of domination by making the contradictions appear as if they are based on natural rather than social distinctions. Fourth, ideology makes appearances take a form directly opposite to proper relations by making it appear as if an economic exchange is the sole object and aim of social relations (Morrison, 1995: 50). Thus, Marx sought to trace the evolution of ideas to the various life conditions at different points in time.

IV. ECONOMIC WRITINGS

Marx's writings on economic aspects of society marked an innovative beginning in social thought. All the works of Marx on economic life are considered to be the most comprehensive contribution to social theory. His first major economic work, entitled *A Contribution to the Critique of Political Economy*, was written in 1859. This work provided an outline of his major economic study of capitalism. The most comprehensive contribution was the three volumes of *Capital* on the origin and history of capitalist society. While Marx had tackled some of the significant elements of capitalist development in *The German Ideology*, he wanted to outline three distinct issues in his study of capitalism. The first issue is that he wanted to look at the historical emergence of commerce as a dominant way of life. The second issue is that he wanted to study the framework of the historical changes taking place in the ownership and use of land and labour that accompanies capitalism. Third, Marx wanted to lay out the fundamental changes in social relations as capitalism was established (Marx & Engels, 1947 (1867): 54-5). Marx divided his significant work *Capital*, Vol. 1 into four parts. Part A deals with the economic and social elements of capitalism. Part B outlines the various aspects of the theory of value. Part C discusses the theory of surplus-value, and finally, Part D concentrates on the genesis of capitalism.

THEORETICAL FOUNDATION OF CAPITALISM

BACKGROUND

The background of Marx's capitalism was based on the notion of 'political economy'. Firstly, the term political economy was discussed and developed by two prominent thinkers, Adam Smith and David Ricardo. Political economy is a school of thought, a branch of economic theory that attempts to explain the structural characteristics of capitalist economies (Marx & Engels, 1947: 55). Thus, political economy was the name given to nineteenth-century economic theory.

Both Smith and Ricardo had written a classic book. Smith was one of the first to describe the fundamental laws of capitalist development in his magnum opus, *The Wealth of Nations*, published in March 1776. This book tried to study the history, causes, and limitations of economic 'progress' or development. Along with Smith, David Ricardo published *Principles of Political Economy* in 1817, and it became the standard economic theory of the day (Smith, 1973). However, Marx's theory of capitalism was primarily concerned with the criticism of Smith and Ricardo's inability to see how economic laws were the effects of much broader historical and social processes.

Marx's critique of Smith and Ricardo took several central questions related to the theory of capitalism as follows: '(i) he disagreed with Smith's and Ricardo's conception of capitalist society as governed by immutable laws and economic functions; (ii) he criticized their tendency to conceive the common good of society as consisting of the private pursuit of economic gain and their conception of society as an interchange between free merchants who exchange labour and wages in the market, (iii) he criticized their work for being indifferent to the economic inequalities inherent in acts of exchange; (iv) he rejected the claim by Smith and Ricardo that value was a 'substance' inherent in commodities; and (v) Marx criticized the political economists for their theoretical methods and their use of abstract categories, which tended to view the economic activity as existing above the practical acts of individuals' (Morrison, 1995: 55-6).

To give a definite shape to the theory of capitalism, Marx made some specific comments on the views of political economists. First, Marx commented on Smith's and Ricardo's assertion that a capitalist economy was autonomous and self-regulating (Marx, 1967 (1867): 100-11). In this sense, society is a set of fixed economic laws that are unalterable. This meant that the low wages and poverty of the working class were also unalterable. Marx thought they had failed to see the interconnections between human activity and economic life in this context. In addition, Marx believed that economic categories were ultimately derived from historical, social relations rather than existing as fixed attributes of a given economic system (ibid., 1973: 100-8). Second, Smith thought that labour and capital were separate, but Marx maintained that they were interconnected. Therefore, to understand capitalism, we first understand the underlying basis of the interconnection between the two and their relationship in a mode of production.

Third, Marx criticized Smith and Ricardo for their tendency to conceive of the common good of society as consisting of the pursuit of private economic gain and for their conception of individuals as free merchants engaged in acts of buying and selling (Smith, 1973: 13). In Smith's view, each individual must pursue monetary gain since self-interest contributes to society's shared prosperity (Morrison, 1995: 55). In response, Marx criticized Smith for being indifferent to the economic inequalities inherent in exchange acts.

Fourth, Marx criticized political economists' view of value. Smith proposed the labour theory of value. According to this theory (Meek, 1973), labour adds value to the commodity, and this value forms part of the substance of the commodity.

In this case, Smith argued that value increases society's wealth and emerges as commodities exchange for a price on the market. In response to Smith's claim that value emerges from the interaction of commodities, Marx believed that Smith had failed to see value as part of a social framework and, therefore, a historical phenomenon.

Fifth, Marx criticized Smith and Ricardo for claiming that the economic activities of production, consumption and exchange could be studied independently. However, Marx thought they were fundamentally related to each other and felt they could only be understood as a system of social relations (Morrison, 1995: 58). In this sense, Marx gave an example by stating, 'A dress becomes a dress only by being worn, and thus, a product is a product, not because it is materialised activity, but only in so far as it is an object for the active subject' (Marx, 1977: 196).

Marx mainly focused on Smith's and Ricardo's one-sided theoretical perspective of economic categories. But, on the other, Marx looked upon these economic categories in their interconnectedness. Thus, for instance, Marx maintained that wealth was not something independently produced outside a mode of production but was inherent in human labour activity (Marx, 1973: 100-5).

THEORY OF CAPITALISM

Understanding Marx's theory of capitalism, looking into five basic concepts and theories is necessary. These are the concept of the commodity, labour theory of value, theory of value, theory of surplus-value, and division of labour.

Concept of Commodity: Commodity is the essential concept or element of the Marxian theory of capitalism. Marx's conception of a commodity was rooted in his materialist orientation, focusing on the productive activities of actors. A commodity, according to Marx, is a thing whose qualities are capable of satisfying needs (Marx, 1967: 125). Thus, a commodity can be seen from two different points of view: its use value and its exchange value. 'Use' and 'exchange' values are central to Marx's theory of capitalism.

The use-value of a commodity may be defined as the particular quality a commodity has to satisfy human needs. In other words, use-value is the ability to fulfil only one specific need or function. For example, a coat provides warmth, the ability of a coat to render heat cannot be affected by another commodity such as bread or coal. These objects are produced for use by oneself or others in the immediate environment (Marx, 1967: 126).

Another form of the commodity is the exchange value. Exchange value, according to Marx, only arises in developed economies, and therefore, is found only in capitalism. The system of exchange is related to the buying and selling of commodities. Instead of producing for themselves or their immediate associates in a capitalist society, the actors produce for someone else (the capitalist) and objects are exchanged in the open money market (Marx, 1967: 35). Exchange value is the capacity of quantities of one commodity to have their value expressed in the form of quantities of another commodity (Morrison, 1995: 61). For example, one ton of rice has the equivalent value of a quarter of a ton of coffee, which means one ton of rice has the exchange value of a quarter ton of coffee.

Marx thought that exchange value is central to the theory of capitalism. First, Marx reasoned that commodities are not comparable to exchange values since each commodity serves a uniquely human function and satisfies a human need. Secondly, Marx thought that 'value in exchange' is historical and is found only in capitalist society and not in other modes of production. Third, since in exchange, use-value disappears because commodities are mutually replicable, all value in capitalist society is expressed in quantitative relation between one commodity and another (Marx, 1967: 126-8).

Fetishism of Commodities: Fetishism of commodities is central to Marx's theory of capitalism. It is crucial to discuss Ricardo's and Smith's views on the labour theory of value. According to this theory, the value of a commodity is created by labour. They focused their arguments on the idea that labour was the sole source of all value, stating that 'it was the real measure of the exchange value of all communities' (Smith, 1973: 44). Contrary to that, Marx argued two points on this issue. First, a commodity only has value concerning some other commodity. Second, that value is part of a social framework rather than a substance that inheres in a commodity (Morrison, 1995: 71).

Marx uses the concept of commodity fetishism to indicate the process whereby individuals assign value to commodities and believe that they have extraordinary power (Morrison, 1995: 72). However, in a capitalist society, commodity fetishism takes a specific shape in the process of exchange. From this perspective, commodity fetishism is historical, and it arises only in societies whose commodities enter into the medium of exchange.

In a capitalist society, dependency relations in a feudal society are replaced by the 'private producer'. "Sometimes Marx refers to the private producer as 'private labour', and in some cases the 'isolated individual'. Whatever the usage, it is key to understanding the system of social relations in capitalism" (Morrison, 1995: 172). In this case, all the characteristics of labour are individual rather than social. All the buying, selling, producing and consuming activities are for private gain and private interest. The exchange process mediates all the relations between individual producers and the rest of society (Morrison, 1995: 170). In this situation, private producers can only find the socially beneficial nature of the labour that they produce. Marx believed that the transactions between material things take on the fetish form at this stage. 'Commodities appear to have a life of their own and enter into social relations with one another, and as such appear to have human qualities' (Morrison, 1995: 76). Fetishism 'is nothing but the definite social relation between human beings which assume the fantastic form of the relation between things' (Marx, 1967: 165). In this way, the fetishism of commodity involves how actors forget that their labour gives the commodities their value. Instead, they believe that value arises from the natural properties of the things themselves or that the impersonal operation of the market provides commodities value. Fetishism, in this sense, brings about a 'fantastic reversal'. Lastly, Morrison has summarized the social effects of Marxian fetishism in the following words:

> Under commodity fetishism, relations among people take the form of the relation among things. At this stage, social life is mediated by what he calls the exchange of matter. In this 'fantastic relation', human beings confront one another as economic subjects—as agents of economic categories and as possessors of commodities. As possessors of commodities, human beings are simply carriers of economic processes and, so long as this is the case, it obscures both their human form and the human form of society. (Morrison, 1995: 76)

Reification: The concept of commodities and fetishism of commodities would have limited sociological use. Therefore, it needs to look at the overall effects of exchange on social relations. Marx referred to this as the process of 'reification'. The basic fact is that people produce economic objects (food, clothing, shelter) and social relationships and, finally, social structure. In this sense, the fetishism of commodities is translated into a broader concept of reification (Lukacs, 1968).

> *Reification* can be thought of as the process of coming to believe that humanly created social forms are natural, universal, and absolute and, as a result, that those social forms do acquire those characteristics. (Ritzer, 1988: 57)

Marx began the discussion of reification by assuming that human beings make society. He believed that the individual and society are unitary things. Because human beings make society, reification reverses this process by appearing as if society gives birth to human beings (Morrison, 1995: 76-7). To the extent that economic functions make it appear that society creates human beings. The concept of reification implies that people believe that social structures are beyond their control and unchangeable. Using this concept, people reify commodities and the whole range of social structures.

Theory of Surplus Value: The concept of 'surplus value' has a significant role in developing capitalism. Two fundamental historical facts are related to the background of the theory of surplus value. First, capitalism has replaced feudalism. As a result, the serfs' relation to the land as a source of livelihood has changed to force serfs to sell their labour as a commodity. Second, in capitalism, the primary aim was to purchase labour at low rates to make more profit.

Here, Marx did not talk about 'profits' but 'surplus value'. For the capitalists to make a profit, they buy 'labour power'. Labour power is different from labour. 'Labour power refers to the capacity of labour to add values to commodities' (Morrison, 1995: 78). On the other hand, human labour is the actual work and physical activity incorporated into the labourer's body (Morrison, 1995: 78). In this context, the capitalist tries to find labour-power in the market as a commodity to make more profit in production. Another reality Marx argued is that labourers could not sell commodities produced by their labour. Still, they must sell the labour-power existing in their bodies as a commodity (Marx, 1967: 272).

In making a profit, capitalists try to purchase 'surplus labour'. In surplus labour 'the workers expand their labour, but this creates no value for them. Instead, they create surplus value with all the charms of something created out of nothing for the capitalist. Hence, I call surplus labour time part of the working day, and to the labour expanded during that time, I give the name surplus labour' (Marx, 1967: 325). Hence, surplus value is defined as 'the quantity of value produced by the worker beyond the necessary labour time, meaning by the latter the working time required to produce a value equal to the one he has received in the form of wages' (Aron, 1970: 165).

Surplus value, therefore, is the value created by surplus labour. Surplus value, as explained by Morrison. According to Morrison (1995: 81), it has four central attributes: (i) it is the value created by the surplus labour of the worker; (ii) it is unpaid and therefore creates value for the capitalist but not the worker; (iii) it presents a deception since it claims to be paid labour; and (iv) it is the recognized form of overwork and thus goes to the heart of the exploitation of the worker in that the worker is not paid for the wealth he or she creates by producing surplus labour.

Theory of Division of Labour: The division of labour is another important structural component of Marx's study of capitalism. Marx and Engels traced the origins of the modern division of labour to the early family, 'where wife and children are the slaves of the husband' (1970: 52). Marx was critical of these early forms of division of labour. His basic view of the division of labour is much concerned with the simple and complex cooperation-based division of labour. Therefore, Marx divided it into two types, viz., the social division of labour and the division of labour in industry or manufacture.

(i) *Social Division of Labour:* This type of division of labour exists in all societies. This is mainly based on exchanging goods between different groups of what that they produce. For instance, some individuals produce food products, cloth products, and various groups produce others. In this context, they fulfil their needs by exchanging these objects. Therefore, these types of societies are considered to be self-sustained and self-dependent.

(ii) *Divison of Labour in Industry or Manufacture:* This division of labour is mainly found in capitalist society. It is based on both simple and complex types of cooperation. In simple cooperation, many workers are brought together in one place for production. Capitalist production then proceeds by unifying many workers and many trades under the command of one capitalist. This is termed, according to Marx, 'the combined efforts of labour' (1967: 443). These combined efforts produce quantitative gains through a qualitative act. Marx believed that the combined cooperation creates a qualitative effect and it concentrates on the means of production in one place (1967: 447). As a result, the entire profit goes to the capitalist. The total value of labour-power is greater than the total sum of wages that the capitalist pays to the workers. Hence, a simple cooperation-based division of labour may be defined as a situation of production in which one capitalist employs many craftsmen who all perform the same work.

Another form of division of labour developed throughout the nineteenth century with manufacturing and industry development and progress. Marx called it 'complex cooperation' (1967: 455-8) of a division of labour based on 'particular cooperation'. According to Marx, complex cooperation occurs when the skills formerly embedded in the worker become functions of the division of labour itself. In this connection, Morrison stated,

> Complex cooperation occurs when each individual performs operations disconnected and isolated from one another and carried side by side. Each operation is assigned a separate craftsman, and the combined action of the cooperators produces the commodity, but no individual craftsmen produce the commodity themselves. In this case, according to Marx, the commodity has gone from being a product of individual craftsman to becoming the social product of the union of craftsmen, each of whom performs only one operation. (Morrison, 1996: 87)

Hence, the breakdown of handicraft skills and the 'decomposition of handicrafts into different and partial operations' (Marx, 1967: 458) took the shape of this type of division of labour. In this way, the division of labour in manufacture completely divorces the worker from his product. This leads to the problems of loss of control, dehumanization and alienation. However, Marx accepted the various aspects of the social division of labour and provided a remedy to tackle the division of labour in manufacture. The only solution, according to Marx, is to establish a communist society so that workers will be able to own and control the means of production. The recognized production process will enable each individual to realize his/her potential and exercise creatively.

V. THEORY OF ALIENATION

Background

Marxian concept of Alienation appeared in his writing the *Economic and Philosophic Manuscript* in 1844. Marx's discussion of alienation occurred in his writing 'Estranged Labour', one of his parts of the manuscript. Alienation denotes the individual's estrangement, and the root cause is the concept of 'Fetishism'. Fetishism suggests that individuals dissociate themselves from their products, whether material things or ideas. In this sense, these products of humanity's creativity are treated as 'fetishes': they are treated as objects of mystery, objects outside people's control. Such objects are thus set apart, they are alien and dominate people.

The concept of 'alienation' occurs in various disciplines, including sociology, social and political philosophy, psychoanalysis, existential philosophy, etc. In addition, it has been used to explain ethnic prejudices, mental illness, class consciousness, industrial conflict, political apathy and extremism.

To understand Marx's theory of alienation, it is necessary to look at the idea of Hegel's alienation. Hegel was the first who introduced the term 'alienation' in his work *Phenomenology of Mind* (1910 [1807]). For Hegel, 'the concept of estrangement demanded an investigation into abstract philosophical concepts and spiritual forces such as consciousness and reason' (Morrison, 1996: 91). Though Hegel believed that the struggle for self-emancipation occurs between self-consciousness and abstract forces in the external world, Marx thought this struggle was acted out on the economic front. Furthermore, for Marx, the struggle for self-realization is a material struggle played out on the economic front, and this shift replaced Hegel's abstract struggle in thought (Morrison, 1996: 91).

The central theme of Marx's theory of alienation is the idea that man has lost control over his destiny and sees this control vested in other entities. In other words, a man who creates society but feels alien from his creation. Marx's primary analytic concern was with the structures of capitalism that cause alienation. Alienation has been described by Coser 'as a condition in which men are dominated by forces of their creation, which confront them as alien powers' (Coser, 1996: 50). Marx discussed four types of alienation: Man is alienated from the object he produces, from the production process, from himself, and the community of his fellows.

(i) *Alienation from the product:* The product of their labour does not belong to the workers, used to satisfy basic needs. Instead, the product belongs to the capitalist, who may use it in any way they wish. Marx rightly stated:

> The object produced by labour, its product, now stands opposed to it as an alien being, as a power independent of the producer. . . . The more the worker expends himself on work the more powerful becomes the world of objects which he creates in the face of himself, the poorer he becomes in his inner life, and the less he belongs to himself. (Marx, 1964: 122)

In short, the worker spends his life and produces everything not for himself but for the powers that manipulate him.

(ii) *Alienation from productive activity:* The second form of alienation discussed by Marx is alienation from productive activity or the process of production. In this type of alienation, 'human beings lose control over the capacity of their labour to affirm their being and define their self-existence' (Morrison, 1995: 3). As Marx puts it,

> However, alienation appears not merely in the result but also in the *process of production*, within the *productive activity* itself. . . . If the product of labour is alienated, production itself must be active alienation. . . . The alienation of the object of labour merely summarises the alienation in the work activity itself. (Marx, 1964: 124)

Workers here do not work for themselves to satisfy their own needs. Instead, they work for capitalists who pay them in return for the right to use the workers in any way they see fit. Thus, Marx identified two 'hostile groups': the 'other man', the capitalist, who commands production, the other the 'proletariat', i.e. working-class or labourers. Once the object is finished, it belongs to the other man, free to use it in whatever manner he chooses.

(iii) *Alienation from himself:* Marx discusses the third type of alienation as alienation from himself/herself. Workers in capitalist society are alienated from their own ***human potential***. At this point, a worker cannot fully develop the many sides of his personality. In this regard, Marx rightly points out,

> Work is external to the worker. . . . It is not part of his nature; consequently, he does not fulfil himself in his work but denies himself. . . . The worker, therefore, feels himself at home only during his leisure time, whereas at work, he feels homeless (Marx, 1964: 124-5). In work (the worker) does not belong to himself but to another person (Marx, 1964: 125). This is the relationship of the worker to his own activity as something alien, not belonging to him, activity as suffering (passivity), strength as powerlessness, creation as emasculation, the *personal* physical and mental energy of the worker, his personal life . . . as an activity which is directed against himself, independent of him and not belonging to him. (Marx, 1964: 126)

Therefore, it can be said that individuals perform less and less like human beings as they are reduced in their work to animals, beasts of burden, or human machines. Alienation from self, thus, takes the form of dehumanization in the spheres of life.

(iv) *Alienation from the community of his fellows:* The fourth type of alienation discussed by Marx is alienation from fellow human beings and the human social community. Marx assumed that 'people basically need and want to work cooperatively in order to appropriate from nature what they need to survive. But in capitalism, this natural cooperation is disrupted, and people, often strangers, are forced to work side by side for the capitalist' (Coser, 1996: 52). In this context, Marx stated:

> Man is alienated from other men. When a man confronts himself, he also confronts other men. What is true of man's relationship to his work, to the product of his work and to himself is also true of his relationship to other men . . . each man is alienated from others. . . . Each of the others is likewise alienated from human life. (Marx, 1964: 129)

Based on the above quotation, it can be said that the worker is alienated not only from himself but from other men, who belong to his community also. Thus, each man is alienated from others, and each of the others is likewise alienated from human life.

In short, Marx thinks that people alienates from one another, from their products, from the process of production, from their society and finally from himself or herself. In a capitalist society, such a system dehumanizes people into a mere commodity, labour, which can be impersonally bought and sold in the labour market. Thus, though alienation exists in all societies with private property of the means of production, Marx argued that only in capitalist society it reached its fullest.

VI. THEORY OF CLASS AND CLASS CONFLICT (STRUGGLE)

Marx has conceptualized the concept of 'social class' and analysed the theory of 'class struggle', which is considered a significant sociological theory contribution. The word 'class' originated from the Latin term 'classic', a group called to arms, a division of the people. Bottomore stated,

> Social classes are *de facto* (not legally or religiously defined and sanctioned) groups; they are relatively open, not closed. Their basis is indisputably economic, but they are more than economic groups. They are distinct groups of the industrial societies which have developed since the seventeenth century. (Bottomore, 1975: 194)

The concept of class structure has been dealt with in the Third Volume of Marx's famous work *Capital* (1894). The central theme of Marx's analysis of social class and class conflict is discovering the principles of change for society. Marx thought that two types of a medium of verbal interaction classes regulated every society. In a capitalist society, these are the 'haves' (owners of land/or capital), often called the bourgeoisie, and the 'have-nots' (those who own nothing but their own labour-power), often called the *proletariat*. Nevertheless, Marx accepted the importance of social class. According to him, 'a social class occupies a fixed place in the process of production'. Two sets of criteria may distinguish members of a social class.

(i) *Objective criteria:* People may be seen to comprise a social class if they have one attribute in common, namely if they share the same relationship to the means of production (Cuff, Sharrock & Francis, 1979: 87). For example, all labourers have a similar relationship with the landowners, so labourers form a social class. On the other hand, as a social class, all the landowners have a similar relationship with the process of production and labourers. In this way, labourers on the one hand and landowners on the other could be seen as classes. However, Marx is not satisfied with this relationship to determine the class. This criterion of class determination is termed a *class in itself*, as discussed by Marx. By *class in itself*, he means the objective criteria of any social class. In this sense, Marx suggests that the basis for social classes might be located in people's different relationships to the means of production. Such relationships crucial to understanding the class structure is termed as, according to Marx, *class for itself* or the subjective criteria.

(ii) *Subjective criteria:* Marx suggested that having a relationship in common is not sufficient to call many people a social class. To classify many people merely in terms of having some common attribute is to do no more than create a *category* (Cuff, Sharrock & Francis, 1979: 88). The members of any one class have similar relationships, but they also share a similar class consciousness. This similar class consciousness becomes a uniting force of its members for organizing social action. According to Marx, this collective action by the class members for their common interest is termed class for itself. In the transformation process from class in itself to class for itself, individuals become part of a concerned class that consciously articulates their common interests.

THEORY OF CLASS STRUGGLE (CONFLICT)

Class struggle is the central theoretical orientation of Marx's writings. The root cause of the development of class struggle is the notion of *surplus value*, the development of *alienation* among labourers and the transformation from 'class in itself' to 'class for itself'. Marx rightly elaborated the theory of class struggle in the following words:

> The history of all hitherto existing society is the history of class struggles. Free men and slave, patrician and plebian, lord and serf, guildmaster and journeymen, in a word, oppressor and oppressed, stood in constant opposition to one another, carried on an uninterrupted, now hidden, now open fight, a fight that each time ended either in a revolutionary reconstitution of society at large or in the common ruin of the contending classes. (Marx & Engels, 1973: 102)

Marx believed that, except in communist society, class conflict is inherent in every differentiated society. There is always a conflict of interests between persons and groups located differently within the social structure in such societies. All human societies have divided classes that clash to pursue class interests. But the fact is that

> modern workers are formally 'free' to sell their labour while being existentially constrained to do so makes their condition historically specific and functionally distinct from that of earlier exploited classes'. (Coser, 1996: 44)

According to this view, the conflict, whether between master and slave, landlord and serfs, bourgeoisie and proletariat, characterized all stages of historical development. However, in the capitalist stage of development, proletariats become conscious of their class position. At this stage, the 'class in itself' transformed into 'class for itself'. Hence, the proletariats acquire the revolutionary character by overthrowing these oppressors that are capitalist or bourgeoisie. In this sense, the factory system becomes the prime locus of antagonism between classes. This factory system makes class the actual self-awareness from self-awareness. Here, 'common struggle takes the position of class as a potential power force'. According to Marx, classes are determined based on an individual's relation to the means of production. These relations are independent of an individual's will. An Individual's class is determined not based on his occupation but the basis of his position relative to the means of production.

In a capitalist society, the means of production and distribution of products are in the hands of the few, and they are called 'haves'. These few people who have the economic power also control political machinery, including the courts, the police and the military. Capitalists also justify their ideology and a political system of domination that serves their collective interest. 'The state is the form in which the individuals of a ruling class assert their common interests. The ideas of the ruling class are . . . the ruling ideas' (Coser, 1996: 78). Thus, political power and ideology seem to serve the same functions for capitalists that class consciousness serves for the working class. At this point, class antagonism acquires the most acute dimensions. The working-class movement gets concretized and reaches its peak. This may turn into a violent revolution destroying the structure of capitalist society. Ultimately, a classless society is likely to be created with the social dictatorship of the proletariat.

Marx's analysis of class and class struggle is mainly considered to critique the capitalist society. The following points are involved in the discussion of the theory of class struggle:

1. *The development of class consciousness among the proletariats:* Marx described this transforming from 'class-in-itself' to 'class for itself'. This transformation only occurs when individuals occupy similar positions based on common interests by developing class consciousness. At this stage, a communication network grows and finally becomes a struggle against the bourgeoisie. Benedix rightly argues as follows:

The first attempts of the workers to associate among themselves always take place in the form of a combination (unions). The large-scale industry concentrates in one place a crowd of people unknown to one another. Competition divides their interest. But the maintenance of wages, this common interest which they have against their boss, unites them in a common thought of resistance-combination. Thus combination always has a double aim, that of stopping the competition among themselves, to bring about a general competition with the capitalist. (1966: 9)

2. *Polarization of classes:* The polarization of classes is the inherent tendency of capitalist society.

Society as a whole is more and more splitting up into two great hostile camps, into two great classes directly facing each other—bourgeoisie and proletariat. (Marx and Engels, 1848: 15)

This is because the bourgeoisie has control over the means of production, and the proletariats are deprived of it. Marx also accepted the division of classes into the small capitalists, the *petit bourgeoisie*, the *lumpen proletariat*, the bourgeoisie, and the proletariat. However, after a certain period, these classes cannot maintain their class position and are finally drawn into the ranks of the proletariat. This is what Aron calls the process of proletarianization, which 'means that, along with the development of the capitalist regime, the intermediate strata between capitalists and proletarians will be worn thin and that the proletariat will absorb an increasing number of the representatives of these intermediate strata' (Aron, 1970: 174). Thus, in the capitalist stage of development, the bourgeoisie and the proletariat become polarized, and conflict occurs between them.

3. *The notion of surplus value:* One of the primary causes of class struggle is surplus value. The capitalists generate this surplus value through the exploitation of labour.

The labour-time necessary for the worker to produce a value equal to the one he receives in the form of wages is less than the actual duration of his work. Let us say that the worker produces in five hours a value equal to the one contained in his wage and works ten hours. Thus, he works half of his time for himself and the other half for the entrepreneur. Let us use the term 'surplus value' to refer to the quantity of value produced by the worker beyond the necessary labour time, meaning by the latter, the working time required to produce a value equal to the one he has received in the form of wages. (Aron, 1970: 165)

In the accumulation of surplus value by the capitalists, the proletariat becomes poorer and poorer. Thus, according to Marx, poverty is not due to scarcity but due to the exploitation of the proletariat class by the capitalist or bourgeoisie.

4. *Pauperization:* The poverty of the proletariat results from the increasing exploitation of labourers by the capitalists. In this process, the bourgeoisie tries to get more profit. Due to this tendency of the bourgeoisie, 'the mass of poverty, of pressure, of slavery, of exploitation' (Abraham & Morgan, 1991: 39) increases among the proletariat.

It follows that in every mode of production which involves the exploitation of man by man, the people who labour are condemned to toil for no more than the barest necessities of life. Sometimes favourable circumstances arise when they can win more, but more often, they get the barest minimum and at times not even that. On the other hand, a minority, the owners of means of production, the property owners, enjoy leisure and luxury. Society is divided into rich and poor. (Cornworth, 1954: 58-9)

Thus, according to Marx, poverty results from exploitation rather than scarcity of resources.

5. *Alienation:* Economic exploitation, the dominance of power, and inhuman working conditions led to the increasing alienation of man. It may be alienation, according to Marx, from the product, productive activity or process of production, fellow human beings, and from himself or herself. Marx rightly points out:

... Within the capitalist system all methods for raising the social productiveness of labour are brought about at the cost of the individual labourer; all means for the development of production transform themselves into means of domination over and exploitation of, the producers; they mutilate the labourer into a fragment of a man, degrade him to the level of an appendage of a machine, destroy every remnant of chosen in his work and turn it into hated toil; they estrange from him the intellectual potentialities of the labour-process in the same proportion as science are incorporated in it as an independent power; they distort the conditions under which he works, subject him during the labour-process to despotism, the more hateful for its meanness; they transform his lifetime into working-time and drag his wife and child under the wheels of the Juggernaut of capital. But all methods for the accumulation of surplus value are at the same time methods of accumulation, and every extension of accumulation becomes again a means for the development of those methods. It follows therefore that in proportion as capital accumulates, the lot of the labourer, be his payments high or low, must grow worse. (Benedix & Lispet, 1966: 10)

Therefore, Man is not free to do work of his/her choice. On the contrary, they are forced to work to fulfil their essential needs. Workers are alienated from the entire production process, product, and finally from their own community in the capitalist society.

6. *Development of class solidarity and conflict:* Due to the transformation from 'class in itself' into 'class for itself', class consciousness among proletariats increases. This leads to integration among the proletariats and provokes them to unite against the bourgeoisie, resulting in a conflict between the proletariats and the bourgeoisie. In the words of Marx:

. . . With the development of industry, the proletariat not only increases in number; it becomes concentrated in greater masses, its strength grows, and it feels that strength more. The various interests and conditions of life within the ranks of the proletariat are more and more equalised, in proportion as machinery obliterates all distinctions of labour and nearly everywhere reduces wages to the same low level. The growing competition among the bourgeoisie and the resulting commercial crisis make the wages of the workers more fluctuated. The increasing improvement of machinery is ever more precarious; the collisions between individual workmen and individual bourgeoisie take more and more the character of collisions between two classes. Thereupon the workers begin to form combination (trade unions) against the bourgeoisie, they club together in order to keep up the rate of wages; they found permanent associations in order to make provisions beforehand for these occasional revolts. Here and there the contest breaks out into riots. (Marx & Engels in Etzione, 1973: 36-7)

7. *Revolution:* The final result of class struggle would be a revolution that will destroy the structure of capitalist society. At the peak of an economic crisis, the conflict between the proletariat and the bourgeoisie becomes violent. In this context, Marx says:

Finally, in times when the class struggle nears the decisive hour, the process of dissolution going on within the ruling class, in fact within the whole range of old society, assumes such a violent, glaring character, that a small section of the ruling class cuts itself adrift and joins the revolutionary class, the class that holds the future in its hands. Just as therefore, at an earlier period, a section of the bourgeoisie ideologists who have raised themselves to the level of comprehensive theoretically the historical movement as a whole. (Marx & Engels in Etzione, 1973: 37-8)

8. *The establishment of a dictatorship of the proletariat and the formation of the communist society:* In the last stage of class struggle, the dictatorship of the proletariats is to be established. The dictatorship of the proletariats ultimately resulted in establishing a classless society, i.e., the formation of the communist society. Irving Howe writes:

By now, almost all socialists have abandoned the treacherous phrase' dictatorship of the proletariat, both because it is open to obvious misconstruction and because it has acquired, in the Stalinist and post-Stalinist dictatorships, abhorrent connotations. Marx himself had written that he differentiated himself from 'those communists who were out to destroy personal liberty and who wish to turn the world into a large barrack or a gigantic warehouse'. (1971: 7)

In short, it can be said that at the peak of an economic crisis, ultimately, a classless society, i.e. a communist society, is likely to be created with the social dictatorship of the proletariats.

VII. THEORY OF SOCIAL CHANGE

Marx's theory of social change is central to all his writings from perspective to theoretical orientation. The notion of social change has been found in every stage of human society. Marx believed that men make their own history. The central theme of Marx's theory of social change, in the words of Coser, is:

> Human History is the process through which men change themselves even as they pit themselves against nature to dominate it. In the course of their history, men increasingly transformed nature to make it better serve their own purposes. And, in the process of transforming nature, they transform themselves. (1996: 55)

The concepts of class struggle, superstructure, substructure, and mode of production are the key to Marx's theory of social change. Class struggle, Marx believed, plays a very crucial role in transformation and social change. To Marx, human history is the history of class struggle. However, the different groups and categories involved in the class struggle differ in different stages of human history depending upon the peculiar mode of production of that period. Therefore, he sees class struggle as the crucial mechanism for changing the social system. In fact, in all stages of human history, two groups are significant: a group with a strong interest in maintaining the existing system and a group with a strong interest in changing it. Social change comes through the struggle—political, legal, economic, and possibly even military—between these two groups.

Marx has discussed two basic structures of society, i.e. the infrastructure or substructure and the superstructure. Marx argues that economy denotes the *substructure* or *infrastructure* of society. The other aspects of society, such as religions, familial and political institutions, are shaped by the nature of the economic base. These different parts he calls the *superstructure* of society. The figure below demonstrates how these concepts are related in the diagrammatic form. Social change theory can be represented as starting at the bottom of the triangle and working upwards to the top.

Based on the above model of society, it can be said that the infrastructure of society plays a crucial role in the process of social change. These changes will automatically bring changes in the superstructure. Marx's theory of social change is applicable in analysing capitalist society. Marx argued that many factors could bring about social change. To bring about a new type of society, the bulk of the population, the free labourers, had to become aware of what was happening in their society. They become an active social group, a social class, based on a common bond, plight and shared identity. Marx called the proletariat, the workers organized as a class in itself and class for itself. The proletariat will overthrow the bourgeoisie at this stage, and the forces and relations will cease to operate. Finally, social antagonism will be replaced by social solidarity in the affairs of human beings. As a result, a classless society will be formed, i.e. a communist society.

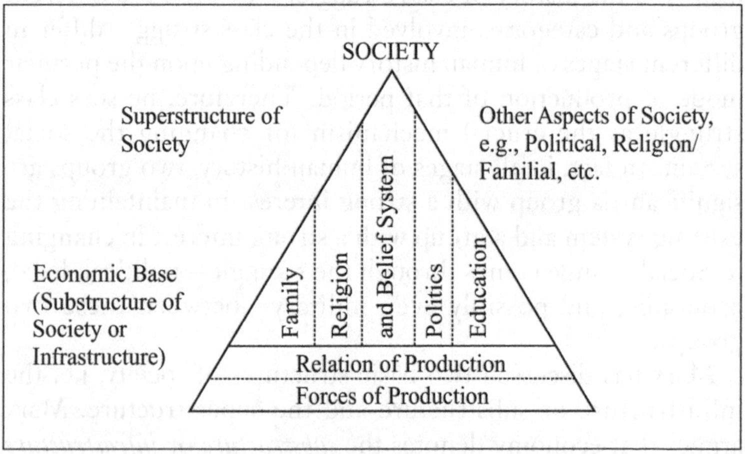

Source: E.C. Cuff, W.W. Sharrock and D.W. Francis, *Perspectives in Sociology*, Unwin Hyman, London, 1990, p. 90.

Figure 2.1: Marx's Model of Society

Marx's analysis of social change is complex in nature and content. Marx's primary concern was to explain the workings of the capitalist system rather than to establish and develop a theory of social change. However, in his thought and writings, the theory of social change has a prominent place to describe and explain the dynamics of social change in all types of society.

VIII. IDEA OF DIALECTICS

The word dialectics refers to a method, intellectual discussion and debate process. Marx was not satisfied with Hegelian idealism, but Hegel's dialectical methodology contributed to Marx's thought. Hegel's dialectics is mainly related to three concepts: thesis, antithesis and synthesis. The *thesis* represents the optimistic view, and the *antithesis* means the opposite or opposing view. Over time, the thesis and antithesis are reconciled in the form of *synthesis*. The synthesis is the composite view. As history progresses, the synthesis becomes a new thesis and then against this new thesis, an antithesis arises and finally turns into a synthesis. And then it repeats every stage of historical development. Hegel applied this understanding of dialectics to the progress of ideas in history. Marx took the dialectical approach in a completely different direction.

In this context, Larson explains,

> To Marx, the matter is not a product of the mind; on the contrary, the mind is simply the most advanced product of matter. Thus, though Marx rejected Hegel's content orientation, he retained his dialectical structure. (1973: 40)

As Marx saw it, the problem with Hegel's thinking was that ideas were the ultimate reality and always the focal point of historical process and change. On the other hand, Marx and Engels believed that motion was the primary existing form of matter (Morrison, 1995: 112-13). Hence, it can be said that Hegel's dialectics was based on 'ideas' while Marx's dialectics was based on 'matters'. Thus, Hegel's dialectical approach is dialectical idealism, while Marx's dialectics is *dialectical materialism*. Let us now discusses Marxian concepts and laws of dialectical materialism.

LAWS OF DIALECTICS

Dialectical materialism tries to explain everything in terms of the contradiction of matter. Dialectical materialism is concerned with the law of reality and abstract laws for natural and social change. Marx's colleagues Frederick Engels put forward the three major laws of dialectical materialism. Engels had propounded these laws in *Anti-Duhring* (Engels, F., 1878: 150-201) and was familiar with Hegelian dialectics. These are as follows:

1. *The Law of the Transformation of Quantity into Quality:* The first law of the dialectic states that one structure can be transformed into another through cumulative change, leading ultimately to qualitative development. According to this law, change is not simple or gradual. Still, it is a product of quantitative advances, which result in abstract qualitative changes at a particular moment when mature conditions are present. For instance, in the natural world, this transformation of matter is found at the level of physical substances, such as when water changes into a solid or when a liquid forms a gas. This change occurs from lower to higher, simpler to complex, and homogeneous to heterogeneous levels of reality.

These changes occur continuously in every object of the natural world into the other when the qualitative change occurs. Moreover, this happens only when new properties accumulate sufficiently to create the 'leap', i.e. the qualitative change. The birth of an infant could be an example of this law. In this process, quantitative changes continue during the gestation period right from conception. Still, qualitative change occurs when the baby breathes in air in this world.

2. *The Law of the Interpenetration of Opposites:* The second law of the dialectic claims that the nature of existence is full of contradiction. Engels believed that these primarily operate in the material world and exist in the form of class contradictions. This law is considered to be the core of dialectics. This law is also called the law of the unity and conflict of opposites. According to this law, there are various internal sides, tendencies, and forces of an object or phenomena that are inseparable, interconnected and opposite in trends. The inseparable interconnections of these opposite tendencies or contradictions are responsible for the unity of opposites. The unity of opposites is a necessary condition of the conflict because it only occurs where opposite sides exist in one object or phenomenon: the contradiction, the conflict of opposites that is the primary source of the development of matter and consciousness. Class struggle and movement are good examples of this law. All movement and struggle arise due to internal contradictions of its sources. This law is also related to the first law which takes qualitative change from quantitative one. This abstract law of unity and conflict of opposites is to be explained and understood if applied to successive modes of production in the history of the development of society.

3. *The Law of Negation of the Negation:* The third law of dialectic assumed its expression in the material world in the form of opposition to the economic and political dominance of the ruling class. Negation arises from its implicit existence and 'develops out of itself elements that end its existence and transform it into its opposite' (Jordan, 1967: 190). Marx believed that negation is an integral part of developing reality itself. He wrote, 'In no sphere can one undergo a development without negating one's previous mode of existence'. For example, in the animal world, each new species of animal, arising based on the old, represents a negation. Therefore, it can be said that negation is the overcoming of the old through internal contradictions. Thus, socialism comes to take over capitalism because it revolves around the internal contradic-

tions of the capitalist society. In addition, a negation of the negative is the second degree of negation in which a new one that is previously overcome by the old is replaced by something newer. The result of this second is again negated, overcome, and so on till infinity. Thus, development appears as countless successive negations, a permanent replacement or overcoming of old by the new.

This law of dialectic can be applied in the development and evolution of various historical stages of human society: primitive communism, slavery, feudalism, capitalism and socialism.

> This development shows that the succession of societies and their system of social relations are interconnected and confirm the underlying process of development described by the materialist dialectic and that its material expression is to be found at the level of economic existence. (Morrison, 1995: 118)

Each historical stage, Marx thought, begins with a mode of production, the economic organization that creates specific conditions leading to a socially dominant class over another. This class structure of society conforms to the laws of dialectical development to the extent that one class negates the other, the other existing to maintain the economic well-being of the class existing over them. In this development process, contradiction and opposition, according to Marx, the negation promotes the subordinate class's cohesion. They form a class whose common conditions of poverty and exploitation constitute a principle of development and change the negation of the negation (ibid.).

In a nutshell, the applicability of the laws of dialectical materialism has been found in every stage of society. In primitive communal society, the conflict between the communal relations of production and the exploiting classes led to qualitative change, i.e. transition into an ancient mode of production. There was a conflict of opposites within the system which led to the negation of the primitive-communal system. After that, a new stage of the slavery system appeared.

The slavery system is described as the negation of a primitive communal system.

In a slave-owning society, there existed contradictions between slave owners and slaves. When it reached the mature stage, the struggle of these contradictions resulted in qualitative change, i.e. the negation of slave-owning society through its transition into a feudal society. The conflict of the opposites, i.e. the slave-owners and slaves, culminated in violent slave revolts, ultimately affecting the negation. It can be said that the feudal system stands as an example of negation of the negation. It means that feudal society can be seen as an example of negating slave-owning society, which denies primitive-communal society. In the feudal stage, the forces of production saw rapid qualitative change. The conflict of opposites within the feudal system, namely, landless serfs against feudal lords, reached maturity.

In a capitalist society, a contradiction was found between the social character of production and the private capitalist form of appropriation. This contradiction or conflict of opposites gives rise to an economic crisis, and employment causes a violent class struggle between the bourgeoisie (the capitalists) and the proletariat (the working class). In other words, quantitative changes. This conflict would integrate the working class, and finally, they make a revolution against the capitalists. This revolution would, according to Marx, abolish the capitalist production of relations and guide the new qualitative change, i.e., the communist socio-economic formation. Hence, according to the law of dialectics, contradictions will remain the basis of development. Thus, it shows how the three laws of dialectics operate in Marx's interpretation of the history of society.

IX. NEW DIRECTION TO MARXIST THOUGHT

During the past four decades, there have been notable changes in Marxist thought in social sciences in general and sociology in particular. As a result, Marxism no longer has the appearance of a body of actual practice but gives direction to the upcoming thought. In a recent development, two principal orientations of Marxist thought have emerged: *Structuralist Marxism* and *Critical Theory*. The former owes its distinctive character to the work of Louis Althusser (Althusser & Balibar, 1970) on the one side and structural linguistics (Robey, 1973) on the other.

Althusser's concerns are primarily epistemological, and he sets out to establish a theory of knowledge in opposition to empiricism. At the same time, he also tries to show the 'scientificity' of Marx's mature theory in contrast to 'ideological' thought. Tom Bottomore has made a comment on Althusser on the lines that he fails to establish two of the main points of his argument—namely, the existence of a total *epistemological break* between the 'Young Marx' and the 'Mature Marx'. In addition, Althusser outlined two main themes in Marx's theory. According to him, Marx's theory:

> reveals the existence of two problems. . . . First, Marx regards contemporary society (and every other past form of society) both as a result and society. Second, the theory of the mechanism of transformation of one mode of production to the succeeding one has to pose and solve the problem of the result, i.e. of the historical production of a given mode of production, of a given social formation. Nevertheless, contemporary society is not only a result, a product; it is this particular result, this particular product, which functions as a society unlike other results and other products which function quite differently. The second problem is answered by the theory of the structure of a mode of production, the theory of capital. (Althusser & Balibar, 1970: 65)

Another side of Marxist thought is mainly concerned with the 'critical theory'. Jürgen Habermas, in his *Legitimation Crisis* (1977), examines the manifestations of economic, political, and ideological crises in late capitalist societies. He, again argues that since the economic system has surrendered part of its autonomy to the state, an economic crisis cannot, in these conditions, directly provoke a problem in the whole social system. Instead, the responsibility of dealing with the problem is assumed by the state, and a crisis of the entire system could only develop if there were a political and an ideological crisis in which the cultural system became incapable of providing the necessary motivations for the maintenance and reproduction of the existing society. In Habermas's view, therefore, the fundamental increasingly tricky problem of late capitalist society is providing an adequate, persuasive *legitimation* of the social order (Habermas, 1976). Bottomore argues the recent growth of Marxist sociology as follows:

> One important reason for the present revival of interest is the fact that Marx's theory stands in direct opposition on every major point to the functionalist theory which has dominated sociology and anthropology for the past twenty or thirty years, but has been found increasingly unsatisfactory. Where functionalism emphasizes social harmony, Marxism emphasizes social conflict; where functionalism directs attention to the stability and persistence of social forms, Marxism is radically historical in its outlook and emphasizes the changing structure of society; where functionalism concentrates upon the regulation of social life by general value and norms, Marxism stresses the divergence of interest and values within each society and the role of force in maintaining over a longer or shorter period of time, a given social order. The contrast between the 'equilibrium' and 'conflict' models of society, which was stated forcefully by Dahrendorf in 1958, has now become commonplace; and Marx's theories are regularly invoked in opposition to those of Durkheim. Pareto and Malinowski, the principal architects of the functionalist theory. (Marx cited in Bottomore, 1974: 304-5)

There has been a close and argumentative relationship between Marxism and sociology for more than a century. The closeness is because Marx's theory was intended to understand the changes in society resulting from the development of industrial capitalism and the political revolutions of the eighteenth century. On the other side, unease and argument arise from how sociology and Marxism developed historically in largely separate spheres. This debate is about whether Marxism is to be conceived as one sociological theory among others or as a unique body of thought. However, the whole intellectual world considers Marxism, a theoretical orientation under sociology, as a radical alternative.

X. CONCLUSION

Karl Marx was a great philosopher and social thinker of the nineteenth century. His contribution is recognized in sociology and other disciplines as a whole. Due to his distinct contribution, a particular school of thought has been established called *Marxism.* Marxist ideas have found a place in almost all social sciences, humanities, and management disciplines. Marx's writings are mainly discussed in two parts: (1) Youthful Marx and (2) Mature Marx. Youthful Marx is primarily known for humanistic thought, while Mature Marx is for scientifically analysed thought. Marx touched upon all the fields or aspects of society. He sees societal evolution through a dialectical approach. His theoretical orientation is also considered evolutionary in practice. Marx's outstanding achievement lies in applying the synthetic approach as he described in a wide-ranging body of work.

Marxist ideas cover a wide range of methodological, conceptual and theoretical orientations in the field of sociology and also in other disciplines of concern. He also gives a direction to revolution. The *Communist Manifesto* is the handbook of revolutionaries around the world. At this point, Marx established a theory of class struggle and the concept of alienation. The notion of alienation and surplus value make a ground for what Marx imagined a class struggle in which finally the socialist type of society would be established. 'History of all hitherto existing societies is the history of class struggle' is the central thrust of class struggle. Marx applied his methodological tool, i.e. *dialectical materialism*, to different historical stages from primitive to capitalist production. This theoretical approach is what he calls *historical materialism.* Due to his theory of class struggle, Marx is considered the father of the conflict approach. At the same time, he also analysed social stratification, family and religion from the viewpoint of conflict approach. Marx argues that religion is opium for society. He, therefore, explained everything from the parameters of two classes—dominant and oppressed. In his theoretical understanding, social change is inevitable in any society.

In a nutshell, Karl Marx is original in thought and approach because he presented a new theory and philosophy that can bring about the emancipation of oppressed people. He struggled throughout his life, based on his experience, and presented a philosophical understanding of social reality. However, his economic emphasis is still relevant in the present context, and his thought seems to be practical in this time and space.

KEY TERMS

Abstraction: An intellectual process using selective perception to reach generalisations. In abstraction, perception is focused on a particular aspect of reality. Common elements may be seen in various objects and events through abstraction, thus facilitating classification and analysis.

Alienation: A feeling of non involvement in and estrangement from one's society, culture and economic activities. The values and social norms shared by others seem meaningless to the alienated individual. Alienation also involves a feeling of powerlessness. The individual feels unable to control his destiny. Meaninglessness involves alienation from values and norms, while the feeling of powerlessness involves alienation from roles. The importance of the concept may be found in the writings of George Hegel, Ludwig Feuerbach, Karl Marx, and Sigmund Freud.

Bolshevism: A branch of *Marxian Communism* developed in Russia under the leadership of Lenin, which gained control of the country in the Revolution of October 1917. The Bolsheviks were concerned with Marxian practical application to their current situation, the development of a disciplined party organization, emphasis upon the indoctrination and leadership of the *Proletariat* by a radical intelligentsia, and the seizure of power by revolution.

Bourgeoisie: The owners of the means of production and distribution in a capitalist society are termed as Bourgeoisie. It ranges from wealthy capitalists to small shopowners. This term is central to Marxian doctrine. Marx regarded the bourgeoisie as a class that controls capitalist societies and suppresses the working class or proletariat.

Capital: Goods or other forms of wealth are not needed for immediate consumption, producing further capital or other goods or services.

Capitalism: An economic system based upon the accumulation and investment of *capital* by private individuals when they become the owners of the means of production and distribution of goods and services. Capitalism is also characterized by economic motivation through private profit, competition, the determination of prices and wages primarily through supply and demand, an extensive system of credit, freedom of contract, and a free labour market.

Class Consciousness: Awareness of belonging to and identification with a given *social class*, accompanied by a feeling of some degree of solidarity with other persons of the same class and the feeling that one's interests are dependent upon the position and attainments of the social class as a whole.

Class Struggle: An inevitable struggle between social classes resulting from their conflicting interests. Both Marxist and non-Marxists use the term to analyse the *conflict theory*. It implies that the process of social stratification engenders potential or actual attempts on the part of whole social classes, or segments of them, to maintain or redistribute existing arrangements of power, wealth, and prestige. Hence, the terms *class struggle* and *class conflict* are often used interchangeably.

Classless Society: A society not divided into a hierarchy of social classes.

Communism: Communism is an ideology concerned with community ownership of all property. It is often used to refer to revolutionary socialism, that is, socialism brought about by revolution rather than gradual evolution, particularly revolutionary socialism based upon the writings of Karl Marx.

Communism, Primitive: A form of *communism* found in certain non-literate societies, in which all the significant economic resources are owned by the community as a whole rather than by any individual, family, kin or other groups.

Conflict Theory: A theory of society that views social phenomena of the past, present, and future resulting from the conflict. Many conflict theorists throughout history, including Heraclitus, Thomas Hobbes, David Hume, George Hegel, Karl Marx, the Social Darwinists, and others. Ralf Dahrendorf sees the conflict model in terms of change, conflict and restraint, resulting in stability, harmony, and consensus in analysing societies.

Determinism: The theory or doctrine in which predecessor conditions and events determine all human behaviour. Determinism is based upon the conception of *cause* and *effect.* It rejects the notion of *Free will* or free choice.

Dialectic: The development of contradictions and their solution to advance the thought of significant influence in modern philosophy. George Hegel's dialectic involves that reality develops through the conflict of opposites, and every action produces a reaction and then an integration or synthesis.

Dialectical Materialism: A philosophical approach of Karl Marx was influenced by Hegel's dialectic approach but rejected Hegel's idealism. Marx emphasized material conditions and economic factors as the primary causal forces determining individual motivation and history. Thus, Hegel's dialectical approach is dialectical idealism, while Marx's dialectics is *dialectical materialism.*

Evolution, Social: A theory of social change based upon the assumption that human societies, in the long run, tend to develop into higher and higher forms. The history of a society is seen as a series of significant stages, each with a more complex level of social organization, a higher ethical character, and a more significant potential for human happiness than the previous. The theory of social evolution is associated with a belief in the inevitability of social progress.

Fetish: Any revered object believed to have a supernatural or magical power to attain the desired ends of someone who possesses or uses it.

Fetishism: A religion that emphasizes the worship of fetishes. It is found in association with *Animism.*

Feudalism: The dominant system of social organization found in Western Europe from the tenth to the fifteenth century. Feudalism was based upon a land tenure system in which land estates of various sizes were given to hold (not to own) by all overloading their vessels (knights) in return for military service. Although the concept of feudalism is based on the model of the feudal society of Western Europe in the later Middle Ages, the term has also been applied to other societies with a similar system of social organization, particularly in medieval Japan.

Historicism: A theoretical approach that emphasizes the importance of historical context in understanding social and cultural phenomena. The emphasis is on the uniqueness of each historical period rather than on recurrent patterns or generalizations from all human behaviour. This approach, influenced by the work of George Hegel, was developed specially by German historians in the eighteenth and nineteenth centuries.

Idealism: A philosophical orientation covering many metaphysical and epistemological doctrines. It views mind or spirit as the ultimate reality or the basis of experience and knowledge.

Ideology: A system of interdependent ideas (beliefs, traditions, principles, and myths) held by a social group or society, which reflects, rationalizes and defends its particular social, moral, religious, political, and economic institutional interests and commitments. Ideologies serve as logical and philosophical justifications for a group's behaviour patterns, attitudes, goals, and general life situations. The elements of an ideology tend to be accepted as truth or dogma rather than as tentative philosophical or theoretical formulations. However, doctrines are modified in accordance with socio-cultural changes.

Industrial Revolution: The radical changes in production and economic production, and social organization resulted from the introduction of power-driven machinery and the consequent rise of the *Factory System.* Industrialization produces a large quantity of material goods that were not available before. The industrial revolution began in England in the eighteenth century and spread to other parts of the world.

Labour Power: A key term in Marx's economic works enabled him to make a central distinction between 'labour' as a human activity and 'labour power' to add value to commodities.

Labour Theory of Value: This theory has been derived from classical political economy. It holds that labour creates the value of any commodity, but the capitalist has the authority over it. Marx was able to show that value is the product of a social framework rather than a substance that inheres to a commodity.

Labour: This term is used in Marx's writings. It describes how human beings produce the means of their existence and their economic survival. Marx took the position that human labour is self-actualizing. Human beings create value through labour, maintain their presence, and confirm themselves in society and history.

Law of Capitalist Accumulation: This law states there is the possibility that the greater the accumulation of wealth by one class, the more there is an occurrence of poverty, misery, and degradation. It demonstrates the doctrine of internal relations by showing that wealth accumulation was not an economic category by itself but took place at the expense of a class whose labour produced this wealth.

Materialism: A term used by Marx and Engels to refer to the theoretical perspective which holds the view that the satisfaction of everyday economic needs is the primary reality. The most basic form of materialism is that society and history are created from productive acts designed to fulfil human needs.

Materialistic Theory of History: This term describes Marx's central theoretical perspective, which explains the laws of historical development and the economic roots of social class and class inequality. The perspective refers to society and history developed in different stages.

Means of Production: The means of production is central to Marx's materialist theory of history. The means of production are anything used to sustain and satisfy material needs in the external world.

Mode of Production: Marx uses this term to identify the primary elements of a given chronological age by showing how its system of production and productive techniques shape its social relations. A mode of production is made up of both 'forces' and 'relations' of production. In each production mode, class divisions arise from property relations that give rights to the owners of the means of production to control both the product and the producer's labour.

Primitive Society: Cultural Anthropologists and Sociologists use the term to refer roughly to cultures that have relatively simple technology, relative cultural homogeneity, and relative isolation from larger cultural influences, whether such cultures have a written language or not.

Proletariat: This term used by Marx refers to a modern type of lower class consisting of wage earners who do not own the means of production but instead sell their labour.

Reification: A term used to denote a stage of social and economic development when human beings experience society as independent of their actions and indifferent to their purpose. Marx used the concept to define society as an objective production while producing human labour.

Relations of Production: This is one of the key concepts of Marx's materialist theory of history. Marx used the term to indicate how a society produces and the social roles allotted to individuals in production.

Revolution: Any change in society brings about fundamental changes, even if they occur over a relatively long time—for example, the Industrial and the French Revolutions.

Social Change: Any modification in the social organization of a society in any of its social institutions or patterns of social class. Usually, social change refers to a significant shift in social behaviour or change in some more extensive *social system* than minor changes within a small group.

Social Class: A large category of people within a system of social stratification who have a similar socio-economic status in relation to other segments of their community or society.

Socialism: An economic and political system based on state ownership and operation of the means of production and distribution. It usually includes rational societal planning to achieve desired goals.

Surplus Labour: This term used by Marx refers to the workday portion that exceeds the amount of labour required for workers to maintain their physical existence and reproduce themselves for necessary food, shelter, and clothing. According to Marx, surplus labour is extracted from the worker and creates wealth for the capitalist.

Surplus Value: Marx used a central concept to identify the form of profit enjoyed by capitalists created from the worker's surplus labour.

Use Value: A central term Marx uses in his discussion of capitalism can be defined as the particular quality of a commodity that has to satisfy human needs. Thus, use value refers to the ability of a commodity to render a specific service to an individual by satisfying some need or want and sustaining life. The use-value of a commodity can fill only one particular function that is not interchangeable with other commodities.

REFERENCES

Abraham, Francis and John Henry Morgan, *Sociological thought from Comte to Sorokin*, Macmillan India, Madras, 1991.

Althusser, Louis and Etienne Balibar, *Reading Capital*, New Left Books, London, 1970.

Aron, Raymond, *Main Currents in Sociological Thought*, Doubleday, Garden City, 1970.

Benedix, Reinhard and Seymour Martin Lipset, *Class, Status, and Power*, Free Press, New York, 1966.

Bottomore, T.B., *Sociology: A Guide to Problems and Literature*, Blackie and Son (India) Ltd, Bombay, 1975.

——, 'Karl Marx: Sociologist or Marxist?', in Serge Denisoff et al., *Theories and Paradigms in Contemporary Sociology*, F.E. Peacock Publishers, Inc., Itasca, 1974.

Bottomore, Thomas, B., *Marxist Sociology*, Macmillan, London, 1975.

Carlyle, Thomas, *The French Revolution: A History*, Chapman and Hall, London, 1896.

Cohen, G.A., *Karl Marx's Theory of History*, Princeton University, New Jersey, 1978.

Colletti, Locio, *Marxism and Hegel*, Verso, London, 1979.

Collins, Randall and Michael Makowsky, *The Discovery of Society*, Random House, New York, 1972.

Cornforth, Maurice, *Historical Materialism*, Lawrence & Wishart, London, 1962.

Cornworth, Maurice, *Historical Materialism*, International Publishers, New York, 1954.

Coser, Lewis A., *Masters of Sociological Thought*, Rawat Publications, Jaipur and New Delhi, 1996.

Cuff, E.C., W.W. Sharrock and D.W. Francis, *Perspectives in Sociology*, Unwin Hyman, London, 1979.

Dahrendorf, Ralf, *Class and Class Conflict in Industrial Society*, Routledge, London, 1959.

Engels, Friedrick, *Anti Duhring*, Foreign Language Press, Peking, (1878) 1976.

Hebermas, Jürgen, *Legitimation Crisis*, Heinemann, London, 1976.

Hegel, G.W.F., *Philosophy of Right*, Clarendon Press, Oxford, 1958.

Howe, Irving (ed.), *Essential Works of Socialism*, Rinehart and Winston, New York, 1971.

Johnson, Doyal P., *Sociological Theory*, John Wiley and Sons, New York, 1981.

Jordan, Z.A., *The Evolution of Dialectical Materialism*, St. Martin's Press, New York, 1967.

Larson, Calvin J., *Major Themes in Sociological Theory*, David McKay, New York, 1973.

Lefebvre, Henri, *The Sociology of Marx*, Vintage, New York, 1968.

Lukacs, George, *History and Class Consciousness*, MIT Press, New York, (1922) 1968.

Marx, K. and F. Engels, *The German Ideology*, International Publishers, New York, (1846) 1947.

——, *Manifesto of the Communist Party*, *Selected Works*, vol. 1, Progress Publisher's, Moscow, (1848) 1969.

——, *The German Ideology: Collected Works*, vol. 5, International Publishers, New York, 1975.

——, *The Holy Family, or Critique of Critical Criticism*, Progress Publishers, Moscow, (1845) 1956.

Marx, K., *A Contribution to the Critique of Political Economy*, Progress Publishers, Moscow, (1859) 1977.

——, *Capital*, vol. 1, International Publishers, New York, (1867) 1967, p. 125.

——, *Grundrisse: Foundations of the Critique of Political Economy*, Middlesex, Penguin, England, (1953) 1973.

——, *The Economic and Philosophic Manuscripts of 1844*, International Publishers, New York, (1932) 1964.

Marx, Karl, *A Critique of Hegel's Philosophy of Right*, J.O'Malley (ed.), Cambridge University Press, (1843) 1970.

——, *Early Writings*, translated and edited by T.B. Bottomore, McGraw-Hill, New York, 1964.

Marx, Karl and Friedrich Engels, 'The Class Struggle', in Amitai Etzioni and Eva Etzioni–Halevy (eds.), *Social Change*, Basic Books, New York, 1973.

——, *The German Ideology*, Part I, C.J. Arthur (ed.), International Publishers, New York, (1845-6) 1970.

Meek, R., *Studies in the Labour Theory of Value*, Lawrence & Wishart, London, 1973.

Morrison, Ken, *Marx, Durkheim, Weber: Formations of Modern Social Thought*, Sage Publications, London, 1995.

Ritzer, *Sociological Theory*, McGraw-Hill Publishing House, Singapore, 1988.

Robey, David (ed.), *Structuralism: An Introduction*, Oxford University Press, Oxford, 1973.

Rotenstreich, Nathan, *Basic Problems of Marx's Philosophy*, Bobbs-Merrill, Indian Polis, 1965.

Rubel, M. and M. Manale, *Marx Without Myth: A Chronological Study of His Life and Work*, Harper & Row, 1975.

Smith, A., *The Wealth of Nations* and D. Ricardo, *On the Principles of Political Economy and Taxation*, Dent, London, (1817) 1973.

Tucker, R.C., *Marx-Engels Reader*, W.W. Norton, New York, 1978.

CHAPTER 3

Herbert Spencer
1820-1903

BIOGRAPHICAL SKETCH

Herbert Spencer (1820-1903) was a leading figure in the intellectual revolution of the nineteenth century. He was a British philosopher and sociologist. Spencer was enormously influential in his own time and played a significant role in developing biology, psychology, sociology, and anthropology.

Herbert Spencer was born in a middle-class family in Derby, England, on 27 April 1820. He was the eldest of nine children and the only one to survive, perhaps one reason he advocated the idea of the 'survival of the fittest' in his theory of evolution. His father, William George Spencer, was a schoolmaster with instructive reformist perspectives. William George Spencer's impact on his child's attitudes and conduct was extensive. Father's non-tyrant training strategies affected Spencer's instructive hypotheses and discipline in the classroom. Spencer's mother, Harriet, exerted little influence on his intellectual development. She was a sweet-tempered, submissive, dutiful, and selfless mother.

Spencer was schooled in technical and practical matters rather than arts and humanities. Spencer was taught at home by his father and uncle. At 16, he went to stay at the home of Uncle Thomas, rector of Hinton Charterhouse in Somerset, for his further study. His uncle, the dissenting clergyman, taught Spencer the principles of philosophical radicalism and the rigid code of dissenting Protestantism. He got his initial education from his father, and his uncle. Spencer did not

Herbert Spencer (1820-1903)

receive any formal instruction in English, and his knowledge of history was superficial. Nevertheless, despite not receiving systematic training, he had good mathematics and natural science background at sixteen.

In 1837, he started to work as a civil engineer for a railway till 1846. Spencer continued to study independently and published scientific and political works during this period. In 1848, Spencer was appointed as an editor of *The Economist*, and his philosophical ideas took shape in a specific direction. During the five years working with *The Economist*, Spencer built up his relations in the world of progressive journalism in London while *Social Statics: the conditions essential to human happiness specified* was published in 1851. In this work, he has presented the core ideas of his sociological theory and a study in political philosophy. During the writing of this work, Spencer began to suffer from insomnia, mental and physical breakdowns, and a series of nervous breakdowns that continued throughout his life. Seven years before Darwin's *Origin of Species*, in 1852, he expounded and advocated a theory of evolution based on Lamarckian principles in his article entitled 'The Development Hypothesis' in the journal *Leader*. It is a pre-Darwinian theory of evolution stressing the notion of the inheritance of acquired characteristics. After his uncle died in 1853, Spencer gave up his job with *The Economist* and lived as a private scholar and a lifelong bachelor.

In 1854, Spencer started writing his second book, *The Principles of Psychology*, published the next year. However, this work did not get satisfactory recognition. After that, he suffered from a nervous illness due to which he could not concentrate on writing and was even unable to read. In 1859, Spencer was influenced by Charles Darwin's book, *The Origin of Species*. He absorbed many of his ideas from Darwin regarding evolution. The views of 'survival of the fittest' and 'natural selection' were fundamental to Spencer's theory of evolution taken from Charles Darwin.

From 1860 and onwards, Spencer wrote several books on concepts, theories, and all-encompassing universal laws. The unification of Spencer's evolutionary theory in 1860 was the culmination of a long period of speculation and the integration of a series of initially unrelated ideas. As expounded in *First Principles*, the perfect theory of evolution, *Synthetic Philosophy*, was published in 1862. In this work, he synthesized a variety of scientific and philosophical thoughts. Spencer expanded and wrote about it in several volumes of *Principles of Biology* written between 1864 and 1867. The *Principles of Biology* is prescribed as a university textbook. After that, *The Study of Sociology* appeared in 1873. This work served Spencer as an introduction to *The Principles of Sociology* and taught him a great deal about sociological methods and objectivity. Early in 1874, Spencer commenced work on *The Principles of Society* and published a multi-volume work in 1896. In addition, a multi-volume work entitled *The Principles of Psychology* was published in 1872. He also wrote many volumes on *The Principles of Ethics* which were published between the 1970s and the 1990s. *The Man Versus the State* appeared in 1884 and *Autobiography* in 1904. In addition, he published several volumes of essays and *fragments* and many volumes of *Descriptive Sociology* (1873-94), mainly written by his secretaries and collaborators. Spencer also advocated the principle of *laissez-faire* or free market, which was popularized by the English economists of his time.

Sociologists of the twentieth century rejected Spencer's work because he did not concentrate and read other people's works. He independently created ideas of his own. Finally, he died as a sad man at the end of his life because he believed that his life work had not achieved its goal as he expected. He died at the age of 83, on 8 December 1903.

I. SOCIOLOGY AS A DISCIPLINE

Herbert Spencer wrote several books on sociology, such as *Social Statics* (1850), *The Study of Sociology* (1873), and *The Principles of Sociology* (1876-96), but he did not give a formal definition of the discipline. According to him, the social process is unique. Therefore, as a science, sociology must explain the present situation of society by explaining the initial stages of evolution and applying them to the laws of evolution. Spencer mainly tried to establish a comparative science of society based on evolutionary principles.

According to his critics, Spencer has taken the idea of a science of sociology from Auguste Comte during his lifetime, and therefore he was indebted to Comte. Spencer denied such allegations and affirmed that he had not read Comte. Like Comte, Spencer believed that order of coexistence and progress characterized the science of society. In this sense, Spencer observed, 'progress from low to high types in individual and social organisms, from the uniformity of structure to multiformity of structures' (1926 [1904]: 488)

Spencer had divided all phenomena of the universe into three categories—inorganic, organic, and super-organic (social) based on the evolutionary framework. According to Spencer, this social science, i.e. sociology, is based on the super-organic, i.e. social evolution.

Spencer discussed the possibility of a science of sociology in *The Study of Sociology* (1873) and accepted that sociology is an actual science based on the positive principle of natural phenomena. However, 'There can be no complete acceptance of sociology as a science', Spencer wrote the possibility of a science of sociology, 'so long as the belief in a social order not conforming to natural law survives' (1961: 360). Here, Spencer emphasized the belief in the social order that has to be discussed based on all other natural laws. To him, social laws are like all other natural laws. In this way, he maintained that causation operates in human behaviour just as it does in different spheres of nature (Sills, 1968: 123).

Spencer also accepted the role of history in the new science, sociology. However, he argues,

> The only history that is of practical value, is what may be called Descriptive Sociology. Moreover, the highest office which the historian can discharge is that of so narrating the lives of nations, as to furnish materials for comparative sociology; and for the subsequent determination of the ultimate laws to which social phenomena conform. (Spencer, 1963: 69-70)

History, according to Spencer, is essentially sociology as it describes past society. Sociology, therefore, is a detailed description of social phenomena in evolution. Thus, the historian and the sociologist can work together to analyse the origin, present structure, and future prognoses of social evolution. All phenomena tend to improve and advance. At this juncture, historians and sociologists have a more significant role in observing, describing, and comparing the nature of social phenomena in evolutionary change. 'The seeds of civilization existing in the aboriginal man and distributed over the earth were certain in the lapse of time to fall here and there into circumstances fit for their development' (Abraham, 1985: 57). It seems that sociology is deeply rooted in the historical study of the process of social evolution and hence social evolution is the key to understanding sociology.

II. THEORY OF SOCIAL EVOLUTION

Spencer is known mainly as a pioneer of evolutionary or evolutionist sociology. He was a contemporary of Darwin, and Spencer had already published theories on this subject before Darwin's *The Origin of Species* (1859). Spencer adopted evolutionary views in the early 1840s and, somewhat disconnectedly, are expressed in his writing on sociological and biological topics through the 1850s (Spencer, 2004: 295). His theory of social evolution was proclaimed in his essay 'Progress: Its Law and Cause' (1857) and honed in *First Principles* (1862).

Spencer's theory of evolution intended to cover all types of the natural process—the development of species, the organic evolution of every animal, the maturation of the embryo, and the evolution of the solar system—besides social development (Peel, 1971: 131). His main aim in propounding the theory of evolution was that human society could be studied scientifically from an evolutionary perspective. He deals with the evolution of phenomena of all classes, from the inorganic to the superorganic. In 1858, Spencer conceived the idea of surveying biology, psychology, sociology, and ethics from an evolutionary perspective (Sills, 1968: 122).

Spencer's entire scheme of knowledge rested upon the belief that 'evolution' was the key concept for understanding the world as a whole and man's place within it. Spencer defined the general process of evolution in the following terms: *Evolution is a change from a state of relatively indefinite, incoherent homogeneity to a state of somewhat definite, coherent heterogeneity* (1958: 367). Thus, his evolution involved increased heterogeneity and indefiniteness, and integration.

Evolutionary sociology passes through differentiation and grouping, and human societies tend to progress from simple to complex forms.

When social density increases, social roles tend to differentiate and split, and the division of labour to increase. But differentiation is not the only mechanism that characterizes the trend from simple to complex. For example, the conquest of territory, integrating one population with another, brings a process of differentiation into the new society that is being created. (Boudon, 1997: 76-7)

The social evolutionary perspective traces the development of human societies from simple to more complex forms with an increasing differentiation of parts and the integration of structure. This evolutionary perspective is also known as a *universal evolutionary theory* because it is not concerned with fixed stages or a unilinear sequence of development. Instead, the universal evolutionary theory accepts the view that the evolution of human society takes place with varying consequences and patterns of different cultures. Spencer has rightly summarized the process of evolution as follows:

Like a lower animal, the embryo of a higher one has few different parts; but it is acquiring greater mass. It is thus with society. At first, the unlikenesses among its groups of units are inconspicuous in number and degree; but, as population augments, divisions, and subdivisions become more numerous and more decided. As we progress from small groups to larger, from simple groups to compound groups, from compound groups to doubly compound ones, the unlikenesses of parts increase. Thus, the social aggregate, homogeneous when the minute, habitually gains in heterogeneity along with each increment of growth, and to reach significant size must acquire great complexity. (Bierstedt, 1974: 563)

Three basic deductive laws are related to the process of evolution. First is the Law of the Instability of the Homogeneous. It states that 'homogeneity is a condition of endemic instability, perpetually under attack from unequal and conflicting forces which ultimately bring about its dissolution, resulting in a progressively intensifying heterogeneity' (Wiltshire, 1978: 197). At the stage of dissolution, there appear no noticeable changes. It is the point of what Spencer called *equilibration*. The equilibration is preceded by 'dissolution'.

The second deductive law is the Law of the Multiplication of Effects. It states that 'every cause produces more than one effect, and that evolution, consequently, perpetually tends towards dissipation. In terms of force, it expresses the universal trend from homogeneity to heterogeneity (Wiltshire, 1978: 197). The third deductive law is the Law of Segregation. It states that 'unlike units of an aggregate tend to separate and like units to cluster, resulting in progressively sharpening structural differentiation' (Wiltshire, 1978: 197). These laws are related to Spencer's work of *First Principles.*

The primary mechanism through which these deductive laws transmit into an organic, animal, and social evolution is natural selection: 'Society advances where its fittest members allow asserting their fitness with the slightest hindrance, and where the least fitted not artificially prevents from dying out (Spencer, 1950: 81). In this sense, the superior can maintain their position on the earth in natural selection in each generation.

The concept of adaptation that appeared early in Spencer's writings is associated with the idea of natural selection. In the process of natural selection, confident individuals and species have the advanced ability to adapt themselves to the conditions of existence. In *Social Statics,* the perfection of man describes a perfect adaptation to the social mode of life. 'The Development Hypothesis' (1853) categorically stated that 'any existing species—animal or vegetable—when placed under conditions different from the previous ones, *immediately begins to undergo certain changes fitting it for the new conditions*' (Spencer, 1915: 3).

The Principles of Sociology (1925-9) describes the operation of the evolution of society. Like all 'organisms', society develops according to individuation, differentiation, and natural selection. 'Between each society and its environment, and between individuals, societies, and races, a process of equilibrium occurs' (Wiltshire, 1978: 202).

Evolutionary terminology is first applied to social growth in 'Progress: Its Laws and Cause' (1857). For instance, differentiation and specialization of function evolve a capitalist economic structure. Then, in *Political Institutions* (1882), these evolutionary categories are applied to political phenomena. Finally *The Principles of Ethics* (Spencer, 1914) relate the process of ethical evolution towards the perfection of 'conduct'. 'Justice describes the evolution of ethics as a development from pre-human to a human state' (Wiltshire, 1978: 205).

Spencer believed that society does not develop through fixed stages; instead, it is based on its social and natural environment. He accepted the role of geography and social history as the determining factors of the evolution of society. He argues,

> While spreading over the earth mankind found environments of various characters, and in each case, the social life fallen into, partly determined by the social life previously led, has been partly determined by the influences of the new environment; so that the multiplying groups have tended ever to acquire differences, now major and now minor; there have arisen genera and species of societies. (Spencer, 1929: 331)

To sum up, all changes have transformation patterns based on their social and natural environment. In this way, the transformation and change take place in the social evolution from:

(i) a condition of simplicity to a state of organized complexity.
(ii) a condition of indefiniteness to a requirement of definiteness.
(iii) a condition of relatively undifferentiated parts to a state of increasing specialization parts.
(iv) from an unstable condition to a stable condition.
(v) relatively incoherent and disconnected behaviour to normal, coherent, and predictable behaviour.

III. THEORY OF ORGANIC ANALOGY

Spencer was interested to apply his idea of social evolution in the investigation of all fields of knowledge. The law of evolution seems to govern societies and the universe, not only the 'supra-organic' but also the organic. In *Principles of Sociology*, Spencer pointed at several analogies between biological organisms and human societies. A society, according to him, is an 'organism', but only in an analogical sense. The notion of balance, differentiation, and an organism applies to both spheres of study.

The 'social organism' concept is central to Herbert Spencer's theoretical contribution. There are two sound interpretations of the term 'organism' which bear a significant relation to the theory of evolution: organism as a functional concept and organism as a physiological one. The former relates to the interaction of the internal components of social and physical structures and compares them (Wiltshire, 1978: 241). By contrast, the body is considered a physical concept in the physiological definition of 'organic' (ibid.). In addition, Spencer also distinguished between 'outer' and 'inner' organs in analysing the social organism. The former is responsible for the relationship of the body with the environment, and the latter for nutrition and distribution (ibid.: 240). In the study of organic analogy, Spencer clearly stated:

> Analogies between the phenomena presented in a physically coherent aggregate forming an individual and the phenomena presented in a physically incoherent aggregate of individuals (forming a society) . . . cannot be analogous between the systems, or methods, of organization. Such analogies result from the one unquestionable community between the two organizations: *there is a mutual dependence of parts in both*. This is the origin of all organizations and determines the similarities between individuals and social organisms. (Spencer, 1966: 411)

Spencer's investigation of the analogy led to the discovery of an impressive catalog of similarities between an organism and society and some significant dissimilarities. In analysing the organic analogy, Spencer traced its roots through the general theory of evolution. He regarded the similarity between society and organisms as the first step toward the theory of organic analogy. In his *Principles of Sociology*, Spencer wrote on the evolutionary understanding of organic analogy. 'So completely is society organized on the same system as an individual,' he argued that we might perceive something more than an analogy between them, the exact definition of life applies to both (biological and social organism). Only when one sees that the transformation passed through during the growth, maturity, and decay of society conforms to the same principles as do the modifications passed through by aggregates of all orders, inorganic and organic is there reached the concept of sociology as a science (Spencer, 1925: 17).

The organic analogy between human society and the biological organism was reformulated by Spencer as follows:

> It is also a character of social bodies, as of living bodies, that while they increase in size, they increase in structure. Like a low animal, the embryo of a high one has few different parts; but its parts multiply and differentiate while acquiring greater mass. It is thus with society. At first, the unlikeness among its groups of units is inconspicuous in number and degree, but as population augments, divisions, and subdivisions become more numerous and more decided. Further, in the social organism as in the individual organism; differentiation ceases only with that completion of the type which marks maturity and precedes decay. (Spencer cites in Abraham, 1977: 217)

In this sense, society views it as analogous to an organism. Thus, the notion of growth is central to both society and organisms.

Spencer developed two straightforward ways to explain the organic analogy between human society and biological organisms. The first type of analogy was the process of evolution from simple to complex forms. In this analogy, species evolve through adaptation, and individual organisms grow and mature. The second line of analogy involved making comparisons between the individual and the social organism from the similarity points of view, an organic analogy can be outlined as follows:

1. Both society and organisms can be distinguished from inorganic matter in terms of growth and development.
2. In both society and organisms, an increase in size increases complexity and differentiation.
3. In both, a progressive differentiation in structure is accompanied by a differentiation in function.
4. In both, parts of the whole are interdependent, with a change in one part affecting other parts.
5. In both, each part of the whole is also a micro-society or organism in and of itself.
6. And in both organisms and societies, the life of the whole is destroyed, but the parts will live on for a while (Spencer, 1974: 22-3).

In comparing the organic analogy, some differences between human society and organisms also need to be outlined. These differences are:

1. Societies have no external forms;
2. The units of societies are not contiguous with one another in a mass;
3. The units of the social organism are spatially mobile; and
4. Societies are organisms that progress through changes similar to that of a living species. (Spencer, 1974: 388-91).

In addition to it, Spencer offers an 'emphatic repudiation of the belief that there is any special analogy between the social organism and the human organism', and he concludes:

> Though in the preceding chapters, comparisons of social structures and functions to structures and functions in the human body have in many cases been made, they have been made only because structures and functions in the human body furnish the most familiar illustrations of structures and functions; in general. . . . Community in the fundamental principles of organization is; thus, the only community asserted. (Spencer, 1898: 613)

In brief, Spencer made a fruitful attempt to establish a theory of organic analogy based on evolutionary principles by making a detailed analysis of similarities and differences between human society and biological organisms. Moreover, in later writings, Spencer used the organic analogy and continued to build his theory of evolution.

IV. EVOLUTION OF SOCIETIES

Spencer's analysis of different types of societies is based on the theory of social evolution. He established the two patterns of making a classification of society. The first is related to the movement from simple societies to various levels of compound societies based on their *degree of composition*. Spencer identified four types of societies in their evolutionary stage—simple, compound, doubly compound, and trebly compound (Abraham & Morgan, 1985: 61).

According to Spencer, the aggregate of some simple societies gives rise to compound societies; the sum of some compound societies gives rise to doubly compound societies (ibid.). Finally, the aggregate of some doubly compound societies gives rise to trebly compound societies (ibid.). According to him, simple societies comprise families, and compound societies comprise families unified into clans, doubly compound societies comprise clans unified into tribes and the trebly compound societies, such as Indian society, have tribes brought together forming nations or states (Timasheff, 1967: 40).

The second type of classification of societies is based on the construction of militant and industrialism. In this type, the evolution of societies takes place from military to industrial societies. These types of classification are also found in many sociologists' works: societies with mechanical cooperation/ societies with organic cooperation (Durkheim), Gemeinschaft/ Gesellschaft (Tonnies), folk/urban society (Redfield), and 'traditional' societies/'modern' societies. A new concept, according to Spencer, can be used here to describe this opposition to 'military' and 'industrial' society.

The words 'military' and 'industrial' are very abstract in Spencer's vocabulary and describe two idealistic limits of an ongoing process characterized by the degree of coercion, maximal or minimal, that a social system, through its various structures and institutions, exerts upon its members. (Boudon, 1997: 77-8)

Spencer's social development account became commonplace in societal contrasts since the mid-eighteenth century, distinguishing between military (Spencer usually used it as 'militant') and industrial societies (Peel, 1971: 192). The principle of the uniformity of natural processes of the small segment of human history gave rise to the distinction between militant-industrial societies in the same direction as the whole span of human evolution and development (ibid.).

Militancy and industrialism are opposed forms of organization that arise in response to existing social backgrounds.

The history of the nineteenth and twentieth centuries shows that the commercial mastery of even a free-trading world rests ultimately upon naval and military power. The modern industrial capitalist state combines the immense technological sophistication, functional integration, and economic profusion celebrated by Spencer with the barbarism, chauvinism, and un-freedom of the 'militant' stage. (Wiltshire, 1978: 252)

Militancy and industrialism exemplify a series of paired opposites: status *vs* contract, vertical ranking *vs* functional role, tradition *vs* innovation, figurative *vs* literal, subordination *vs* equality, the command economy *vs* the free market, deliberation *vs* spontaneity, and so forth (Peel, 1971: 207). Therefore, militancy and industrialism are opposites that dominated classical sociology in terms of a contrast between a static political realm and a dynamic economic realm.

Military society is characterized by predominant offensive and defensive military action based on compulsory cooperation. Spencer rightly points out, 'The military type is one in which the army is the nation mobilized, while the nation is the quiescent army, and which, therefore, acquires a structure common to army and nation' (Spencer, 1898: 577). Efficient fighting requires clear collective goals and centralized control to coordinate men to achieve them, then transferred them to civil tasks (Peel, 1971: 205-6). The community tends to have 'precise gradations of rank . . . and complete submission of each rank to the ranks above it' (Spencer, 1898: 578). In a militant society, goodness equates with bravery, strength, and military virtues. Based on the above discussion, we can outline the following characteristics of the militant society:

(i) military action is predominant;
(ii) human relationships are marked by compulsory co-operation;
(iii) goodness is equated with bravery, strength, and military virtues;
(iv) based on a specific structure that is a highly centralized authority and social control pattern;
(v) military structure based on a ranking that shows the hierarchical nature of society; and
(vi) state domination of all social organizations.

In the military society, individuals exist for the benefit of the state. On the other hand, industrial society characterizes an independent voluntary organization, a relatively open system of stratification, and decentralized forms of government based on human production and welfare for the society. To explain the central features of the industrial society, Peel observes:

> The industrial cooperation paradigm is provided by relations in trading transactions, between employers and workers, or buyers and sellers. The essence is voluntary cooperation as the judgments and interests of the participant individuals dictate so that there is 'unchecked power of forming associations' that rule themselves on democratic principles in industrial societies. There is a minimum of collective or corporate tasks for whose attainment individuals are disciplined, but all tasks are left to be performed by voluntary associations. (1971: 206).

In an industrial society, a state exists for individuals and a more stable community. It confers freedom and a self-regulating social conscience. 'Being carried on by voluntary cooperation instead of by compulsory cooperation, industrial life as we know it habituates men to independent activities and leads them to enforce their claims while respecting the claims of others' (Spencer, 1950: 133).

Based on the above discussion, we can outline the following characteristics of industrial societies:

(i) military activity and organization is peripheral to society;
(ii) these societies concentrate on human production and welfare for the people;
(iii) state exists for the sake of a more stable community;
(iv) growth of free associations and institutions;
(v) these societies are marked by voluntary cooperation and are regulated by independent voluntary organizations;
(vi) a relatively open system of stratification;
(vii) a decentralized government controls these societies;
(viii) separation of the economic realm from political control of the government; and
(ix) association with duty and labour ideas. 'The industrialism of modern life has strongly associated the ideas of duty and labour' (Wiltshire, 1978: 250).

The inventors of the military and industrial dichotomy were themselves closely involved with the transformation of society. Spencer's primary concern is that the 'gradual development of industrialism was a shift in men's characters from the egoism of the savage to the altruism of the forward spirits of the modern age. The way forward lay in the completion of these changes' (Peel, 1971: 200). Despite his attempt to classify the societies based on evolutionary principles, these societies cannot fit into either of the systems. They only served to make a model for classifying societies based on 'social evolution'.

V. FUNCTIONALISM AND INDIVIDUALISM

Herbert Spencer is considered both a functionalist and an evolutionist. Function, for Spencer, is inevitable for society, and this school became the centre stage of theoretical orientation in sociology. He wrote in 1876 in Volume III of his *Principles of Sociology* on the utility and usefulness of function. In his words, 'There can be no true conception of a structure without a true conception of its function' (Spencer cites Abraham & Morgan, 1985: 66). At the same time, society has a more significant role to play in the benefit of its members. Spencer states, 'The society exists for the benefit of its members; not its members for the benefit of society . . . the claims of the body politic are nothing in themselves and become something only in so far as they embody the claims of its competent individuals' (Spencer, 1925: 449-50). Thus, the individual in Spencerian theory gets maximum freedom and self-determination in the interests of societal progress.

In Spencer's analysis, structure and function are interdependent and interlinked. Spencer emphasized that a change in the profile of a structure occurred with the change in its function. He rightly points out that changes in structure cannot happen without changes in functions. If an organization consists of such a construction that its parts can carry on mutually-dependent actions, then the proportion as an organization is high; there must be dependence on each part upon the rest so great that separation is fatal. This truth is equally well shown in the individual and social organisms (Spencer, 1966: 473).

Spencer was, by nature, not only a functionalist but also an individualist. There are many essential components necessary for determining the characteristics of society, and that fundamental characteristic is the individual. In this regard, Spencer conceived that society would work as a vehicle to enhance individual purposes. Spencer stated,

Just that kind of individuality will be acquired which finds in the most higher organized community the fittest sphere for its manifestations. The ultimate man will be one whose private requirements coincide with public ones. He will be that manner of a man who, in spontaneously fulfilling his nature, incidentally performs the functions of a social unit. (1954: 483)

The best society is a society that least controls the individual. For the functionalist approach of Spencer, if society is to evolve into higher and more advanced social structures and functions, it must move from the simple to the complex activities of a society related to the movement from the lesser military stage to the more industrial societies. Although the relationship between the individual and society is problematic and complex, the relation between man (or animal) and his constituent cells is the equivalent of the link between society and its constituent cells (men). It is an analogy of scale and strongly suggests the continuity of all phenomena.

VI. CONCLUSION

Herbert Spencer was a leading figure in the intellectual revolution of the nineteenth century. Spencer was considered the second founding father of sociology only after Auguste Comte. Spencer was enormously influential in his own time and played a significant role in developing biology, psychology, sociology, and anthropology. Unlike Comte, who wanted to guide men in constructing a better society, Spencer instead desired to show people through sociology that human beings should not interfere with the natural processes that are going on in societies.

Spencer's thought was revolutionary in approach and had a strong belief in the notion of 'the survival of the fittest'. In this sense, Darwin influenced him. Spencer argues that the fittest people are healthy and more intelligent. His evolutionary approach provided the solution for many of the dilemmas faced by the intellectuals at the time. Spencer discussed both social evolution as well as a natural evolution. In social evolution, he described the involvement of two processes. First, the movement from simple societies to various levels of compound societies in terms of four evolutionary stages—simple, compound, doubly compound, and trebly compound. Second, there is a change from the military (or militant) to industrial society. Natural evolution, to him, is the subject of all universal phenomena—inorganic, organic, and super-organic.

An organic analogy is one of the crucial works of Spencer. Spencer tries to establish a relationship between human society and biological organisms by comparing and outlining the differences. He considers society as a super-organic entity, that is, an organizational entity over and above the level of the organism. Nevertheless, his understanding of the super-organic nature of society has several problems. He was unable to see culture as part of an integrated whole. His explanation regarding the social evolution of societies from simple to compound, and so on, is also considered faulty. Timasheff accepts his theory as a philosophical theory rather than a sociological one.

Despite several problems in his thought, Spencer has got a pioneering position in sociology. His popularity extended not only to England but also to the United States and Russia. His ideas became famous because of his desire to unify knowledge and explain scientifically. Spencer, therefore, has succeeded in raising the status of sociology to that of a science of society.

KEY TERMS

Compulsory Cooperation: This kind of cooperation among people is compulsorily imposed by the leaders who represent authority.

Darwinian Theory of Evolution: The idea that man evolved gradually from animal ancestors through genetic mutation and natural selection resulting from the survival of the fittest, the persistence of those organic changes that provide the most significant competitive advantage for survival in a particular environment. It is applied to men also.

Evolution: The theory that all existing plant and animal life forms developed gradually to complex forms from earlier and simpler forms.

Evolution, Social: A theory of social change based upon the assumption that human societies, in the long run, tend to develop into higher forms. The theory of social evolution was associated with a belief in the inevitability of social progress.

Freewill: The doctrine that the individual has freedom of choice in determining his actions and that factors beyond his control do not entirely predetermine his behaviour.

Functionalism: Society is a system of interrelated parts in which no part can be understood in isolation from the whole. The development of functionalism is based on the model of the organic system found in the biological sciences.

Heterogeneous: Heterogeneous denotes the composition of unlike elements.

Homogeneous: Homogeneous refers to the composition of like elements.

Laissez-faire: A doctrine, policy, or ideal holding that government should not interfere with economic activity or control.

Organisms: The view that society is structurally similar to a biological organism. Society is viewed as being essentially analogous to a human or animal system, with its independent parts (or organs) making up the totality of the body of society.

Social Darwinism: The attempt to apply the evolutionary theories of plant and animal development to explain social phenomena.

Voluntary Cooperation: This kind of cooperation among people is not imposed on them but is voluntarily accepted.

REFERENCES

Abraham, Francis and John Henry Morgan, *Sociological Thought From Comte To Sorokin*, Macmillan India, Chennai, 1985.

Abraham, J.H., *Origins and Growth of Sociology*, Penguin Books, New York, 1977.

Bierstedt, Robert, *The Social Order*, McGraw-Hill, Inc., New York, 1974.

Boudon, Raymond, *Herbert Spencer in The Classical Tradition in Sociology: The European Tradition*, vol. II, edited by Raymond Boudon, Mohamed Cherkaoui, and Jeffrey Alexander, Sage Publication, London, 1997.

Peel, J.D.Y., *Herbert Spencer: the evolution of a sociologist*, Heinemann, London, 1971.

Sills, David L. (Editor), *International Encyclopedia of the Social Sciences*, vol. 15, The Macmillan Company and The Free Press, New York, 1968.

Spencer, Herbert, 'The Development Hypothesis', vol. 1, pp. 1-7 in Herbert Spencer, *Essays: Scientific, Political and Speculative*, Appleton, New York, (1852) 1915.

——, *An Autobiography*, vol. 2, Watts, London, (1904) 1926.

——, *Education: Intellectual, Moral, and Physical*, Littlefield, Paterson, N.J., (1854-9) 1963.

——, *First Principles*, DeWitt Revolving Fund, New York, (1862) 1958.

——, *Social Statics: The Conditions of Human Happiness Specified, and the First Developed*, Routledge, London, (1850) 1954.

——, Specialized Administration, vol. 15 (pp. 401-44) in Zeller, Osnabruck (Germany), The Works of Herbert Spencer, (1871) 1966.

——, *The Man Versus the State*, 2nd edn., Watts, London, (1884) 1950.

——, *The Principles of Ethics*, 2 vols., Appleton, New York, (1892-3) 1914.

——, *The Principles of Sociology*, vol. 2, Appleton, New York, 1898.

——, *The Principles of Sociology*, 3 vols., Appleton, New York, (1876-96) 1925-9.

——, The Social Organism quoted from Jonathan H. Turner, *The Structure of Sociological Theory*, The Dorsey Press, USA, 1974.

——, *The Study of Sociology*, University of Michigan Press, Ann Arbor, (1873) 1961.

——, *The Works of Herbert Spencer*, Otto Zeller, Osnabruck, vol. I, *Essays: Scientific, Political and Speculative*, (1855) 1966.

Timasheff, Nicholas S., *Sociological Theory: Its Nature and Growth*, Third Edition, Random House, New York, 1967.

Wiltshire, David, *The Social and Political Thought of Herbert Spencer*, Oxford Historical Monograph, Oxford University Press, Oxford, 1978.

CHAPTER 4

Emile Durkheim
1858-1917

BIOGRAPHICAL SKETCH

Emile Durkheim (Lukes, 1973), one of the pioneers in sociology, was born in 1858 at Espinal in France. He was considered one of France's greatest social thinkers and academic sociologists who developed sociological concepts, methodology, theories, etc. He graduated from the École Normale. Durkheim taught sociology at the University of Bordeaux and then lectured on education and sociology in the Sorbonne from 1902 until he died in 1917.

The core of Durkheim's approach is termed *sociological realism.* Durkheim has emphasized the ultimate sociological reality of the group rather than the individual. Here, he states that society is 'suigeneris', i.e. a reality in itself. In keeping with the tradition of nineteenth-century thinkers, such as Saint Simon, Auguste Comte, Spencer, etc. Durkheim also believed that this new science of society (sociology) must be studied and interpreted based on natural sciences methods and approaches.

I. THE DIVISION OF LABOUR IN SOCIETY

Durkheim's first major theoretical work was *The Division of Labour in Society*. It was written during the 1880s as a doctoral thesis and was later published as a complete study in 1893. While becoming more autonomous, Durkheim's central question is: why do individuals depend more upon society? (Durkheim, 1964: 37).

Emile Durkheim (1858-1917)

Durkheim's main focus in *The Division of Labour* is on *social solidarity*. Social solidarity is the condition within the group where there is social cohesion and cooperation. The collective action aims to achieve group goals, and social organization is shown by permanency. These conditions are changeable according to social situations. Due to this reason, Durkheim proposes two types of solidarity, i.e., *mechanical* and *organic*.

Societies whose solidarity is mechanical are based on shared roots of identity, similarity, undifferentiated social structure and little or no division of labour (Durkheim, 1964). In these types of societies, the individual is directly linked to society through various attachment points, which bind all the members of the group together equally. The force of these social links is to discourage individual autonomy. The social whole envelops the individual so entirely that there is no distinction between individual and collective conscience (Durkheim, 1964: 152). Mechanical solidarity can be characterized by a segmental social structure with a relatively low moral and material density volume. According to Durkheim, when interactions occur among limited people it is called *volume*, whereas the number of times people interact is also limited (*density*). The fundamental criterion of mechanical solidarity is collective conscience, and collective conscience develops from the homogeneity of experience and gives rise to common beliefs and practices. Durkheim has defined it as thus:

> The totality of beliefs and sentiments common to average citizens of the same society forms a determinate system with its own life; one may call it the collective or common conscience. (Durkheim, 1964: 79-80)

In brief, societies of this type are characterized by:

(i) a small and homogeneous population which is isolated; (ii) a division of labour based on social cooperation, with little or no specialization; (iii) a system of social institutions in which religion is dominant; (iv) a system of beliefs which is uniformly diffused throughout the society, creating uniformity in attitudes and actions; (v) a low degree of individual autonomy; (vi) a social organization in which the individual's place in society is determined by kinship; (vii) a system of penal law based on repressive sanctions which punish individual transgressions swiftly and violently, serving the function of reaffirming core beliefs and values; (viii) a system of social cohesion which produces a high degree of consistency in values and beliefs, and in individual attitudes and actions; (ix) a state in which individualism is at its lowest point of development; and (x) a system of social links between individuals based on custom, obligation and sentiment (Morrison, 1995: 129-30).

In contrast to mechanical solidarity, the other form of social solidarity, as Durkheim refers to it, is *organic solidarity*. Solidarity in industrial or modern society is based not on uniformity but differences is termed 'organic solidarity'. In societies with organic solidarity, labour is specialized, and individuals are linked. The nature of these links, Durkheim reasons, stems from the development of the division of labour, where individuals become more reliant on others to perform separate economic functions that they cannot carry out themselves (Durkheim, 1964: 182). Society is an arrangement of different functions linked mutually by social bonds. In the division of labour, the advancement of society through progressive development leads to a decline in the intensity of collective behaviour. The content of collective conscience gradually becomes human-oriented, secular and rational. These social situations start weakening the values of collectivity.

In brief, organic solidarity is characterized by an increase in the density of society due to the expansion of population, the growth of cities, and the development of means of transportation and communication. The major characteristics of organic solidarity are: (i) larger populations spread over broader geographic areas; (ii) an increased complexity of the division of labour leading to specialized economic functions in which individuals are more reliant on others to perform economic functions which they cannot perform themselves; (iii) a system of social relations in which individuals are linked to each other by contract rather than by sentiment and obligation; (iv) a system in which individuals obtain their place in society by occupation rather than by kinship affiliations; (v) an increased individual autonomy based on a system of laws recognizing rights and freedoms of individuals; and (vi) the development of contract law predicated on restitutive sanctions in which judicial rules redress social wrongs by restoring things to their original state (Morrison, 1995: 131).

Durkheim identified two different societies which correspond to mechanical and organic forms of solidarity. These are segmental societies that resemble mechanical solidarity, and advanced societies correspond to organic solidarity.

Durkheim used *segmental* to describe a society of small groups linked together in a defined social territory (Durkheim, 1964: 175). Morrison explained the characteristics of segmental societies: (i) they are made up of small groups or segments separated into tribes; (ii) they have proximity to each other; (iii) they have a division of labour which patterns their activity so that links of cooperation develop between the segments along domestic and political lines; and (iv) they produce strong social bonds between the segments which are formed by social relations based on shared beliefs and social practices that have their roots in religious laws (Morrison, 1995: 139). This serves to produce a system of social practices that creates common customs and social rules which provide almost total social cohesion. Moreover, their solidarity is mechanical because they share underlying traits, have similar beliefs and values, and are defined by their religious beliefs. In this sense, their social bonds tie the individual directly to society (Durkheim, 1964: 180).

The structure and function of advanced societies are substantially different from segmental societies. The main characteristics of advanced societies based upon the size of the population, the proximity of cities and the development of the division of labour. Generally, advanced societies have greater social density among the overall population, spreading out over a larger geographical area. In such circumstances, the total mass of society is more significant in scope and, therefore, more differentiated (Durkheim, 1964: 181-2). Social differentiation is more developed in advanced societies than in segmental societies, and it results in a complex division of labour. In this context, Aron points out,

> Social differentiation, a phenomenon characteristic of modern societies, is the formative condition of individual liberty. Only in a society where the collective consciousness has lost part of its overpowering rigidity can the individual enjoy certain autonomy of judgement and action. In this individualistic society, the major problem is maintaining that minimum collective consciousness without which organic solidarity would lead to social disintegration. (Aron, 1970: 24)

This type of society is mainly related to the occupation of the individual. Hence, individualism is at its highest point of development and individuals are generally grouped by occupation rather than by kinship. Durkheim accounted for the emergence of advanced or organic societies based on society's growing 'volume'. He pointed out that expansion, both territorially and demographically, increased the physical density of the population and therefore added to its social density, i.e. greater communication and interaction.

LEADING CAUSES OF DIVISION OF LABOUR

The transitions from segmental to advanced societies are central to the development of the division of labour. Durkheim believed that labour division begins when the social, economic and political boundaries dividing segments breakdown, and segments come together. Then, as the segments become more and more 'permeable', they become less resistant to change, creating movement between the parts of the social groups (Durkheim, 1964: 174, 256-82). Instead of dispersed social life over separate segments, it becomes more consolidated and localized, increasing society's moral density (Morrison, 1995: 143). Hence, the division of labour arises due to increased material and moral density in society. By material density, Durkheim meant the sheer increase in the number of individuals in a society, in other words, ***population growth***. By ***moral density***, he means the increased interaction between individuals due to growth in numbers.

Durkheim tried to explain three primary causes of the division of labour. Firstly, the change in individuals' geographical proximity means that the population concentrates in limited areas instead of being spread over larger territories. This 'presupposes a certain tightening' in the social fabric as its human element comes closer together and more geographically proximate (Durkheim, 1964: 258). Second is the 'formation of cities', which occurs as the social density increases

(Durkheim, 1964: 258). These cities create an intensification of interaction between individuals leading to an increase in the overall social mass. Second, as the social group increases, it accelerates the mixing of segments into consolidated social organs. The third is the increase in social volume. This results when the growing social mass produces more frequent communications and transportation. Finally, this new form of interchange acts to 'suppress gaps' between segments, leading to increased moral density, intra-social relations, and frequency of contact between individuals (Durkheim, 1964: 259-60).

ABNORMAL FORMS OF DIVISION OF LABOUR

In the last and concluding section of the Division of Labour, Durkheim focuses on abnormal or pathological forms of division of labour. The term pathology derives from the biological sciences and is primarily used to indicate disease in an organism. Durkheim believed that the 'social body', like the human body, can become diseased, and he referred to this state as a form of social pathology or, more commonly, *abnormal forms* (Durkheim, 1964: 353).

In the third volume of Division of Labour, Durkheim categorized three abnormal division of labour forms found in advanced societies. These are (i) the anomic division of labour, (ii) the forced division of labour; and (iii) the poor coordination of functions resulting from the division of labour itself (Durkheim, 1964: 389).

The first abnormal form of division of labour is the *anomic division of labour*. Durkheim believed that this division of labour arises because of industrial and commercial crises. According to Durkheim, these occur when 'social functions are not adjusted to each other' (Durkheim, 1964: 354). In this context, individual does not feel integrated into society. Social norms and values seem unclear and unintegrated, and the individual does not feel morally involved with the affairs of society.

Moreover, in modern industrial societies, where specialized functions and operations occur, individuals no longer feel that their common work unites them (Durkheim, 1964: 368). Anomic division of labour, it seems, is the incomplete development from mechanical to organic solidarity through the development of industrial society.

The second form of social pathology is the process Durkheim referred to as the *forced division of labour* (Durkheim, 1964: 374). This type of division of labour arises from external inequality that fails to produce the natural demands of society. Thus 'people might be allocated positions in the division of labour to which their natural talents or their abilities do not suit them' (Craib, 1997: 69). An individual may thus become frustrated and unhappy with society under abnormal form. Consequently, the division of labour no longer meets the social needs of cohesion but instead serves the interest of certain social groups (Durkheim, 1964: 374-84). The Indian caste system is one of the examples of forced division of labour.

The third abnormal form of division of labour arises from the poor coordination among various functions of society. 'It is a managerial deficiency, where the enterprise is not organized to get the best, and most out of its members—the more continuous and coordinated the various functions, the more solidarity grows, and the more skilled the workers become' (Craib, 1997: 69).

In brief, Durkheim's study of the division of labour brings out his functional model of society. Durkheim investigates the division of labour as a process that would help individuals coexist and cooperate. In a 'normal' situation, the division of labour contributes to social integration by giving each individual a specialized activity to perform. Division of labour arises due to the competition for survival brought about by growing material and moral density. The specialization offers a way whereby various individuals may coexist and cooperate. Thus, Durkheim does not merely look at the economic aspect of the division of labour but its social aspect, its contribution to social integration.

II. THE RULES OF SOCIOLOGICAL METHOD

Durkheim's second major work, *The Rules of Sociological Method*, was written between 1893 and 1894 and was published in 1895 (Durkheim, 1938). This work is a methodological study by Durkheim. Its primary aim is to outline the nature of sociology and set out the steps of sociological investigation. By and large, *The Rules of Sociological Method* covers four areas of inquiry:

> (i) it identifies the nature of social subject matter by putting forward a definition of social facts and collective representations; (ii) it outlines the rules to be used in observing social subject matter; (iii) it sets out criteria for making judgements about healthy and unhealthy societies; and (iv) it identifies a system for classifying societies according to their structure and complexity, a process Durkheim referred to as *social morphology*. (Morrison, 1995: 151)

Durkheim had three aims in writing *The Rules of Sociological Method*. First, he wanted to establish social realities outside the individual and investigate these realities by scientific methods. Second, he wanted to make sociology independent of philosophy by replacing speculative thought with factual observation. Durkheim, like Comte before him, wanted to change sociology from a science of existence to a science of things and thereby establish a factual basis for the existence of social phenomena, thus eliminating any further need to 'speculate into their reason for being' (Durkheim, 1938: xxxvii). Third, he tried to set out what he thought was the specific subject matter of sociological investigation.

The main thrust of Durkheim's methodology is *social facts*. Social phenomena are *social facts*, and these social facts are the subject matter of sociology. 'They have, according to Durkheim, distinctive social characteristics and determinants, which are not amenable to explanations on the biological or psychological level' (Coser, 1996: 129). Durkheim defined social facts as follows:

> A social fact is every way of acting, fixed or not, capable of exercising on the individual an external constraint; or again, every way of

acting which is general throughout a given society, while at the same time existing in the right, independent of its manifestations. (1938: 13)

Based on the above definition, three distinct characteristics of social facts can be outlined: (i) they are 'general throughout society' and 'diffused within group'; (ii) they are 'external to individuals' and exist independently of their will; and (iii) 'they exercise external constraint over individuals which is recognized by the power of external coercion, by the existence of some sanction or by the resistance offered against individual efforts to violate them' (Morrison, 1995: 155). This category of facts, wrote Durkheim, 'consists of ways of acting, thinking and feeling, external to the individual and endowed with the power of coercion by reason of which they exert control' (1938: 3). He says, 'These ways of thinking could not be confused with biological phenomena, and thus constitute a new variety of phenomena to which the term "social" ought to be applied' (ibid.).

After defining the characteristics of social facts, Durkheim turned his attention toward various rules involved in social facts as a methodological tool as follows:

(i) Rules for the observation of social facts.
(ii) Rules of distinguishing between Normal and Pathological Social facts.
(iii) Rules for the classification of social types.
(iv) Rules for the explanation of social facts.

RULES FOR THE OBSERVATION OF SOCIAL FACTS

Durkheim outlined five general rules for the observation of social facts. The first social facts are to be considered as *things*. As 'things' means that these must be studied by the empirical method and not direct intuition, a simple effort of the will cannot modify them. Second, Durkheim maintained that social phenomena must be considered social facts for the adequate observation of social facts; social phenomena must be considered distinct in themselves and separate from 'consciously formed impressions' in mind. It means the objectivity of social facts depends on their being separated from individual facts which express them. Therefore, when a sociologist undertakes the investigations of some order of social facts, he is supposed to consider them independent of their manifestations. Third, according to Durkheim, social facts must never be looked upon as products of individual will but rather should be looked at as capable of shaping actions by external coercion (Durkheim, 1938: 29). The fourth rule of observation states that to consider social facts as they are, we merely adjust our way of observing things to confirm their nature (ibid.). Fifth, Durkheim thought that social facts are viewed as having independent existence. Therefore, all social facts must be treated independently of individuals and thus be considered part of a world whose regularity and patterning exist independently of psychological characteristics (Durkheim, 1938: 45).

To encounter the problems in observing social facts, Durkheim outlined several steps. First is the procedure of eradicating all preconceptions when observing social facts. This serves to maintain objectivity and eliminate any presuppositions inherent in the mind. Second is the importance of the definition of things to be investigated. This helps the function of defining the subject matter that is to be known. The third is ensuring that the subject matter studied is always made up of phenomena defined by external characteristics (Morrison, 1995: 157).

RULES OF DISTINGUISHING BETWEEN NORMAL AND PATHOLOGICAL SOCIAL FACTS

Having discussed social facts' rules, Durkheim distinguishes between 'normal' and 'pathological' social facts to describe healthy and unhealthy societies. Durkheim explains a social fact is considered normal when understood in the context of the society in which it exists. He further adds that a social fact that is 'general' to a given society is 'normal' (Durkheim, 1938: 64). Thus, social facts are normal when widespread or general in society. For example, crime is considered a normal social phenomenon because it is found in all societies in one form or another. He used the concept of 'normal' to imply that those social phenomena that could be so-called were necessary to operate a 'healthy', well-ordered society (Cuff et al., 1990: 34). Thus, crime is considered normal, which is found in all societies. Therefore, it is acceptable in any healthy society.

Crime is considered a normal social phenomenon. He demonstrated this by first asking how general crime is (Durkheim, 1938: 65). Crime, he stated, is present, not in most societies but in all societies. First, therefore no society is exempt from the problem of crime. Second, as societies progressed from simple to complex, the number of crimes declined in proportion to the population. Hence, though still normal, crime tends to lose its character as normal the more complex society becomes. Third, statistical records enable us to follow crime rates historically, and they tend to increase according to the development of city life. Fourth, no phenomenon more rapidly demonstrates normality than crime since crime is a common condition of collective life. Thus, in Durkheim's view, crime is 'normal' (Morrison, 1995: 159). The conclusion can be drawn that crime is a factor of 'social health' and an integral part of healthy societies. He accepted the sociological role played by crime in society.

Durkheim used the term *morbidity* for pathological states of a living organism. Thus, Durkheim uses the term morbidity to refer to anything that impairs society's functioning by induced diseased states. He stated that 'for societies as for individuals, health is good and desirable; disease, on the contrary, is bad and avoided' (Durkheim, 1938: 49). Durkheim also suggests that though some social facts may be general in society, they may not really 'fit the conditions for that society'. Therefore, he modified the simple condition of generality with the condition that the social fact had to be 'bound up with the general conditions of the collective life' of that particular type of society, in that specific stage in the evolution or development of society. Using the concepts of 'normal' and 'pathological', Durkheim appears to be coming close to making value judgements about 'good' or 'bad' for a society. In this context, a crime is considered both normal and pathological. It becomes an abnormal or pathological fact if the crime rate exceeds the convention of society.

RULES FOR THE CLASSIFICATION OF SOCIAL TYPES

After discussing the rules of distinguishing normal and pathological social facts, Durkheim classified societies according to the nature and type of their organization. Classification of societies into types is an essential step towards explaining problems. *Social morphology* is used for the classification of social types. 'Social morphology refers to the study of the form and structure of societies and how these structures may be classified according to their various social attributes' (Morrison, 1995: 160). Durkheim believed that social morphology is the first principle of social classification since it examines the most elementary forms of society.

There are two broad morphological classifications: first, societies whose organization is simple. These societies have few parts, and the relationship between the parts leads to an uncomplicated structure. Second, there are societies whose organization is complex. These societies have multiple parts, forming more complex structures leading to a more variegated social life (ibid.). Durkheim maintained that the procedures for classifying society should be based on understanding the morphology of simple societies. Therefore, Durkheim looked at the characteristics of simple societies. These have two primary structural attributes: they form a whole whose functions are not dependent on other parts and have no regulating centre. The first example of this type of society,

Durkheim suggested, is called a 'horde' (Durkheim, 1938: 82-3). A 'horde' is the most elementary social form characterized by the fact that it 'contains a single segment' (Durkheim, 1938: 82). Durkheim defined 'the horde is a social aggregate which does not include any other more elementary aggregates or group but is directly composed of individuals' (Durkheim, 1938: 83).

As referred to by Durkheim, the next morphological type is called a 'clan'. The clan may combine various hordes or groups whose union creates a more complex group structure (Morrison, 1995: 161). Another type of classification Durkheim referred to is 'polysegmental'. These societies are made up of a combination of many groups, which form an entire social structure (ibid.). A union of polysegmental societies would result in more complex societies called 'polysegmental societies doubly compounded' and so on.

Analysing Durkheim's procedure of classifying societies into social species or types, John Rex examines the usefulness of this 'biological approach to sociological investigations'. He finds cases where biological approaches would be helpful in sociological investigations and become complex. Difficulties occur in the biological approach to sociological investigations when history becomes the subject of study. In such cases, 'species' is discovered by authors out of the historical process, and a theory of evolution is less helpful (Rex, 1961: 14).

RULES FOR THE EXPLANATION OF SOCIAL FACTS

In chapter five of *The Rules of Sociological Method*, Durkheim explained social facts. In this context, Durkheim suggests two approaches for presenting social facts—the causal and the functional. The former is concerned with explaining 'why' the social phenomenon in question exists. The latter involves establishing the 'correspondence between the fact under consideration and the general needs of the social organism, and in what this correspondence consists of' (Durkheim, 1938:

95). Before that, Durkheim made a distinction between functions and causes. Briefly, 'functions' are distinct from causes because they explain the utility or purpose that a social fact helps. Causes, on the other hand, explain how facts have 'originated' (Durkheim, 1938: 90).

Hence, Durkheim suggests that in explaining social facts, investigators should (a) find the causes of social facts and (b) find the functions of social facts. 'In the search for causes, the sociologists should look for antecedent social facts, that is, those social facts which precede and seem to produce the particular social facts under investigation. In the search for functions, he should look to the "*general needs*" of the social organism' (Cuff et al., 1990: 35).

Having discussed the two approaches to explaining social facts, Durkheim turned his attention to understanding the method by which the nature of social facts can be determined to present these facts. In this way, Durkheim draws a sharp line between the individual and society and between psychology and sociology. An attempt to explain social facts directly in terms of individual characteristics or terms of psychology would make the explanation false. Therefore, in the case of causal explanation, 'the determining cause of a social fact should be sought among the social facts preceding it and not among the states of the individual consciousness'. In the case of functional explanation, 'the function of a social fact ought always to be sought in its relation to some social end' (Durkheim, 1938: 110).

The final point is about Durkheim's logic of explanation in his stress on the comparative nature of social science. Durkheim rightly points out 'we have to compare cases in which they are simultaneously present or absent, to see it the various ways they are present in these different combinations of circumstances indicate that one depends on the other' (Durkheim, 1938: 125).

Durkheim, in the last, discussed the relevance of the comparative method in the analysis of the science of society. According to Durkheim, 'Comparative sociology is not a particular branch of sociology; it is sociology itself, in so far as it ceases to be purely descriptive and aspires to account for facts' (Durkheim, 1938: 139).

In this context, Durkheim wanted to use a comparative method for the analysis of society by making comparisons: (i) of variations of a phenomenon in different parts of society; (ii) of variations of a phenomenon in different societies at a time; and (iii) of variations of a phenomenon among different societies at different times.

In brief, Durkheim's discussion on *The Rules of Sociological Method* tries to find a scientific method to study the science of society. In this regard, he identified social facts and laid down rules for their observation, classification and explanation. In addition, he also focused on the approaches to explain social facts and the logic of explanation. Finally, in the rules of the sociological method, Durkheim outlined the various types of society and, lastly, the relevance of the comparative method in the field of social sciences.

III. DURKHEIM'S THEORY OF SUICIDE

Durkheim started to work on the problem of suicide in 1888 while he was at Bordeaux. His interest in the situation was aroused while working on an article related to suicide and the birth rate (Lukes, 1973: 191). After completing this work, he offered a series of public lectures on this topic between 1889 and 1890 and later, in 1897, his third major sociological work, entitled *Suicide*, was published. The research reported on *suicide* (1897/1951) can be seen to use the ideas developed in *The Rules of Sociological Method.* In suicide, he demonstrated that social facts, particularly social currents, are external to and coercive of the individual.

Durkheim's attempt to formulate a social theory of suicide led him to look for the cause of suicide within the framework of society rather than in the psychological states of individuals. He put this clearly when he stated that 'the causes of death are outside rather than within us and are effective only if we venture into their sphere of activity' (Durkheim, 1951: 43).

Thus, the suicidal act, 'which at first seems to express only the personal temperament of the individual, is the supplement and prolongation of a social condition which they express externally' (ibid.). The shift from psychological to social factors is stated by Durkheim as follows:

> When suicide is considered an individual action affecting the individual only, it must depend exclusively on individual factors, thus belonging to psychology alone. Is not suicide's resolve explained by his temperament, character, antecedents and private history? Instead of seeing in them separate occurrences, unrelated and separately studied, the suicides are taken as a whole. In that case, it appears that this total is not simply a sum of independent units but is a new fact *sui generis*, with its unity, individuality, and consequently its nature—a nature, furthermore, more dominantly social. (1951: 46)

Durkheim, as a sociologist, was not interested in studying why any specific individual committed suicide. That was to be left to the psychologist. Instead, he was interested in explaining differences in suicide *rates*; that is, he was interested in why one group had a higher rate of suicide than another (Ritzer, 1988: 78). For the analysis of suicide rates, Durkheim gave the concept of the *social suicide rate* (Durkheim, 1951: 51). The 'social suicide rate' is a term used by Durkheim to refer to the number of suicidal deaths in a given society and the extent to which the 'rates' themselves could be looked upon as establishing a pattern of suicide for a given society. Durkheim arrived at the concept of the social suicide rate by a careful examination of mortality data which he obtained from public records of societies such as France, Prussia, England, Denmark and Austria. These records contained information about the cause of death, age, marital background, religion, and the total number of deaths by suicide of the country that gathered them (Morrison, 1995: 165). Durkheim assumed that biological, psychological, and social-psychological factors remain constant from one group to another or from one time.

Thus, if there is variation in suicide rates from one group to another or from one time to another, Durkheim assumed that the difference would be due to variations in sociological factors, particularly social currents (Ritzer, 1988: 78). Moreover, these sociological factors would be different social characteristics, religions, patterns of family life, military obligations, and thus, suicide characteristics.

To Durkheim, the critical factors of suicide rates were found in differences at the level of social facts. There are two types of social facts—*material* and *non-material*. Material social facts occupy the position of causal priority but not of causal primacy. Thus, for example, Durkheim looked at the significance of dynamic density. 'Dynamic density refers to the number of people in a society and the amount of interaction that occurs among them' (Ritzer, 1988: 74). Differences in suicide rates found that its effect is indirect. However, differences in dynamic density (and other material social facts) affect differences in non-material social facts, and these differences directly affect suicide rates. In this connection, Durkheim made two related arguments. First, he argued that different collectivities have different collective consciences and collective representations. These in turn, produce different social currents, which have differential effects on suicide rates. Second, Durkheim argued that changes in collective conscience led to changes in social currents, leading to changes in suicide rates. In other words, changes in suicide rates are due to changes in social facts, primarily social currents (Ritzer, 1988: 79-80).

TYPES OF SUICIDE

Durkheim has propounded a theory of suicide divided into two explanatory parts. In the first, Durkheim explained suicide based on social integration. Integration refers to how collective sentiments are shared or the strength of the social bonds between the individual and society. Here, egoistic and altruistic suicide form opposite poles of social integration, i.e., altruistic suicide is associated with a high degree of integration and egoistic suicide with a low degree of integration. Durkheim explained suicide based on social regulation in the second part of the theory.

In contrast to integration, social regulation refers to the restraints imposed by society on individual needs and wants, i.e. the degree of external constraint on people. Here, anomic and fatalistic suicide form opposite poles of social regulation, i.e. fatalistic suicide is associated with high regulation while anomic suicide is with low regulation. Pope (1976: 12-13) offered a handy summary of the four types of suicide discussed by Durkheim by interrelating high and low degrees of integration and regulation as follows:

Social Integration	Low—Egoistic Suicide High—Altruistic Suicide
Social Regulation	Low—Anomic Suicide High—Fatalistic Suicide

EGOISTIC SUICIDE

The term 'egoism' originated in the nineteenth century and was widely used by Durkheim and others to indicate the breakdown of social ties. Egoism can be described as how individuals detach themselves from society by turning their activity inward and retreating into themselves (Durkheim, 1951: 279). Egoism is characterized by excessive self-reflection on personal matters and a withdrawal from the outside world. Egoism occurs, according to Durkheim, because of the tie binding 'the individual to others is slacked and not sufficiently integrated at the points where the individual is in contact with society'. As a result, egoism results from too much individuation and the 'weakening of the social fabric' (Durkheim, 1951: 279-81). 'When men become "detached from society" when they are thrown upon their own devices and loosen the bonds that previously had tied them to their fellows, they are prone to egoistic, or individualistic, suicide' (Coser, 1996: 134).

Hence, high rates of *egoistic suicide* are likely to be found in those societies where the individual is not well integrated with the collectivities or groups as a larger social unit. On the other hand, firmly integrated families, religious groups and politics act as agents of astrong collective conscience and discourage suicide. Durkheim puts it in terms of religious groups as follows:

Religion protects man against the desire for self-destruction . . . what constitutes religion is the existence of a certain number of beliefs and practices common to all the faithful, traditional and thus obligatory. Therefore, the more numerous and strong these collective states of mind are, the stronger the integration of the religious community, also the greater its preservative value. (1951: 170)

For example, Catholics show far fewer suicides than Protestants, regardless of race and nationality. In this context, Durkheim stated that 'the superiority of Protestantism concerning suicide results from its being a less strongly integrated church than the Catholic Church' (1951: 159).

Family, like religious groups, is a second powerful counter agent against suicide (Durkheim, 1951: 171-202). Non-marriage increases the tendency to suicide, while marriage reduces the danger by half or more. In addition, family life reduces egoism by ensuring that greater commitment concentrations are focused within the family rather than on the individual. This in itself, acts to suppress the tendency to withdraw to the self (Durkheim, 1951: 180).

A political or national group is the third powerful counter agent against suicide (Durkheim, 1951: 202-8). This is a more obscure category than either religion or the family. According to Durkheim, political society refers to social bonds between individuals and society. It encompasses the links that develop between individuals and their national groups. Durkheim reasoned that to the extent that these social links exist, it is possible to look at how they are manifested in the suicide rates during times of social crisis and political upheaval

(Morrison, 1995: 175). Based on collected facts, Durkheim outlined that instead of breaking social ties, the severe social disruption brought about by a political crisis increases the intensity of 'collective sentiments and stimulates patriotism' (1951: 208). This, as a result, increases social integration between the individual and the group and 'causes a stronger integration of society' (ibid.).

ALTRUISTIC SUICIDE

The second type of suicide discussed by Durkheim is altruistic suicide. This kind of suicide results from the over-integration of the individual into his social group. Firstly, Durkheim made his observations about altruistic suicide by looking at tribal societies. He observed that social customs in these societies placed a high degree of social honour on individuals who take their own lives in the name of social purposes greater than themselves. In this category, Durkheim lists three specific types of suicides: (i) the suicide of older men threatened with severe illness; (ii) the suicide of women on the deathbed of their husbands; and (iii) the suicide of followers on the death of their chiefs (1951: 219). Under these circumstances, people take their own lives not because they take the personal right to do so but because a social duty is imposed upon them by society (ibid.).

Some examples of altruistic suicide are women throwing themselves at the funeral pyre of their husbands (known as sati in India); Danish warriors killing themselves in old age; the Goths jumping to their deaths from high pinnacles to escape the ignominy of natural death; suicide of followers and servants on the end of their chiefs. In addition, Japanese Hara-kiri, self-immolation by Buddhist monks, self-homicide by army suicide squads and self-destruction in Nirvana under Brahminic influence illustrate other altruistic suicides.

Altruistic suicide is at the opposite pole of social integration, is egoistic suicide. In egoistic suicide, there is excessive individualism and autonomy, whereas in altruistic suicide, little or no individuation occur. In egoistic suicide, the bonds between the individual and society grow weak, which takes its toll on individual life; in altruistic suicide, the bonds between the individual and society are developed to such an extent that the individual acquires an aptitude for the renunciation of life (Durkheim, 1951: 221).

Durkheim argued that altruistic suicide takes several different forms and discussed three distinct types: (i) obligatory altruistic suicide, (ii) optional altruistic suicide, and (iii) acute altruistic or mystical suicide (ibid.: 222-3).

(i) Obligatory altruistic suicide where society imposes an explicit duty on individuals to take their own life. Still, this duty may lack specific coercive pressure from the community.

(ii) In optional altruistic suicide, the community's demand placed on the individual is less explicitly clarified or 'less expressly required' than in circumstances where suicide is strictly obligatory.

(iii) In the third category, acute altruistic suicide, the individual renounces life for the actual felt 'joy of sacrifice'.

Hence, altruistic suicide results from an excess of social integration and is at the polar extreme of egoistic suicide. Therefore, the cause of altruistic suicide is excessive social integration that leads to a lack of development of individualism.

ANOMIC SUICIDE

The last type of suicide discussed by Durkheim is anomic suicide. Anomic suicide occurs when the regulative powers of society are disrupted. Thus, anomic can be defined as the decline in the regulatory authorities of society. Durkheim first used the concept of anomic in the *Division of Labour* in 1893. Durkheim attributed anomic suicide to unlimited aspirations and the breakdown of regulatory norms. He believed that the causes of deregulation could be traced to two primary sources: (i) the development of industrial society; and (ii) the dominance of the economy over other institutions (Durkheim, 1951: 254-8). Thus, any abrupt transitions such as economic disaster, industrial crisis or sudden prosperity can cause deregulation of the normative structure. That is why, Durkheim reasons, anomic is a chronic state of affairs in the modern socio-economic system.

FATALISTIC SUICIDE

Durkheim's fourth type of suicide is fatalistic in a footnote of his writing *suicide*. Durkheim stated that anomic suicide is more likely to occur when regulation is too weak, whereas fatalistic suicide is more likely to happen with excessive regulation (ibid.: 276). Durkheim described those more likely to commit fatalistic suicide as 'persons with futures pitilessly blocked and passions violently choked by oppressive discipline' (ibid.). As an example of fatalistic suicide, Durkheim cited the suicide of slaves who take their own lives, seeing no alternative to enslavement under the master.

In brief, Durkheim put forward three concepts making up a social theory of suicide: egoistic, altruistic, and anomie. The first two suicides, egoistic and altruistic, explain suicide by looking at the social attachment framework that Durkheim called social integration. On the other hand, the third concept, anomic suicide, belongs to a framework that explains suicide takes place in changes in the regulatory mechanism of society—egoistic suicide results from the lack of integration of the individual into his social group. The first type of suicide occurs due to overdeveloped individualism, while the second is due to a lack of development at the individual level. Anomic suicide, in contrast, occurs because of the reduction of the regulatory mechanism of society. Thus, fatalistic suicide has little relevance in the real world. In this study, Durkheim displayed an extreme form of sociological realism.

IV. *THE ELEMENTARY FORMS OF THE RELIGIOUS LIFE*

Durkheim's fourth major sociological work is *The Elementary Forms of the Religious Life*, written between 1902 and 1911 and published in 1912. This work is often regarded as the most profound and original writings of Durkheim. This text is a 'second-hand' study of the religion of Australian aborigines. Durkheim never went to Australia but used the studies of those who investigated these tribes first-hand, with some additional evidence from studies of Native Americans (Craib, 1997: 70). However, this study is based on the description and detailed analysis of the clan system and totemism present in the Arunta tribe of Australian aborigines. He assumed that all the essential aspects of religious life would be visible in the simplest religious forms. The simplest was totemism, found in societies closest to 'the beginning of evolution'.

Durkheim began with the reigning theories of the origin of religion. Tyler and Spencer supported the notion of *animism*, i.e. spirit worship as the most basic form of religious expression. Max Mueller put forth the concept of *naturism*, i.e. the worship of nature's forces. Durkheim observed in his theory of religion that men have never worshipped any other reality throughout history, whether in the form of the totem or God. The collective social reality is transfigured by faith (Abraham & Morgan, 1985: 119). Buddhism and Confucianism recognize no central god or deity.

FUNDAMENTAL AIMS OF THE WORK

Durkheim's theory of religion has five central aims. The first is to study primitive religion and explain its basic structure. This, Durkheim believed, would lead to an understanding of religion and the religious nature of society. The second aim, according to Durkheim, is to arrive at an understanding of contemporary religions by going back to the most primitive.

He believed that only by going back to the earliest religious institutions can we understand the nature of religious life. The third aim of the study is to examine religion from the perspective of positive science. This is based on the rejection of earlier views on religion, i.e. animism and naturism. This he thought, led to the discovery of most elementary forms of religious life. Finally, the fourth aim of the study is to look into the relationship between religious ideas and the organization of bodies of knowledge and systems of classification (Durkheim, 1965: 8). Finally, the fifth aim is to demonstrate that religion is nothing more than the expression of society consecrated when reduced to its basic elements (ibid.).

CENTRAL THEME OF THEORY OF RELIGION

Durkheim paid attention to two central parts or elementary forms, searching for religion's definition and central theme. First, he said that all religions could be defined as a system of beliefs and rites.

> The term 'elementary forms' is misleading. Stated simply, the term refers to the fundamental features (composite elements) underlying religions and religious phenomena. The two elementary forms of religion put forward by Durkheim are: (i) a system of beliefs and rites which specifies attitudes taken up toward the world; and (ii) the division of things into sacred and profane. (Durkheim, 1965: 36)

Beliefs refer to a set of ideas and attitudes held concerning sacred things, whereas rites are defined as a system of action developed toward religious things or objects. The second is that all religions can be explained by their tendency to divide the world into two types of phenomena, the *sacred* and the *profane*. This division of the world 'into two domains, the one containing all that is sacred, the other all that is profane, is the most distinctive trait of religious life' (Durkheim, 1965: 37-47).

SACRED AND PROFANE

The division between sacred and profane is the central principle of the social theory of religion, and it is the most distinctive element of religious life. Durkheim believed that the sacred and profane form the basis of religious life.

> The sacred refers to things human beings set apart, including religious beliefs, rites, deities, or anything socially defined as requiring special religious treatment. Participation in the sacred order, such as in rituals and ceremonies, gives a special prestige, illustrating one of the social functions of religion. (Abraham & Morgan, 1985: 120)

In this context, Ritzer puts it,

> Durkheim concluded that society is the source of all religion. Society (through individuals) creates religion by defining certain phenomena as sacred and others as profane. Those aspects of social reality are described as sacred—set apart and deemed forbidden—from the essence of religion. The rest are defined as profane—everyday, the commonplace, the utilitarian, the mundane aspect of life. The sacred brings out an attitude of reverence, respect, mystery, awe, and honour. The respect accorded to certain phenomena transforms them from the profane to the sacred. (Ibid., 1988: 85)

The profane, according to Durkheim, is considered as opposed to the sacred. In this respect, the profane is subordinated in dignity to the sacred. The profane can contaminate the sacred, and hence the sacred and profane are linked together. Durkheim mainly outlined six characteristics of the sacred and the profane. First, the sacred is always separated from all other objects and therefore constitutes things set apart. Second, rites and social practices systems arise which sets out how the sacred is to be approached and how members of the group are to conduct themselves in the presence of the sacred object (Durkheim, 1965: 37-41). Third, sacred things are protected by interdictions with the force of prohibitions or taboos acting to protect and isolate the sacred. Fourth, sacred things are separated from profane things and are superior in dignity. Fifth, the sacred and the profane represent a unifying principle that separates the natural from the spiritual world and provides society with a model of opposites such as good and evil, clean and dirty, holy and defiled, etc. (Durkheim, 1965: 40). Sixth, a passage from the profane to the sacred must be accompanied by rites thought to 'transform' one state into the other through rituals of initiation or rebirth (ibid.: 39-41).

To give a specific definition of religion, Durkheim believed that three conditions are essential for the development of religion. First, there must be a development of a set of religious *beliefs*. Second, these beliefs are 'the representations that express the nature of sacred things and the relations they sustain, either with each other or with profane things' (ibid.: 56). Third, a set of religious *rites* is necessary. These are 'the rules of conduct which prescribe how a man should conduct himself in the presence of these sacred objects' (ibid.). Finally, religion requires a *church* or a single overarching moral community. The interrelationships among the sacred, beliefs, rites and church led Durkheim to the following definition of a religion:

> A religion is a unified system of beliefs and practices relative to sacred things, that is to say, things set apart and forbidden beliefs and practices which unite into one single moral community called a church, all those who adhere to them. (Ibid.: 62)

Let us now discuss Durkheim's understanding of elementary forms by considering totemism, which forms the central part of the study.

DURKHEIM'S STUDY OF TOTEMISM

To explain the more complex religions of the world, Durkheim believes one must understand first the simple forms. Instead of animism and naturism, Durkheim took the notion of 'totemism' among the Arunta tribe of Australian aborigines as the key concept to explain the origins of religion. Durkheim maintained that totemism is the simplest form of religion.

Totemism (Durkheim, 1965: 102-19) is linked with a clan, a social organization of the clan. The members of the clan believe that they have descended from some common ancestor. This could be an animal, a plant or even some non-living object. The 'common ancestor' is the 'totemic object'. Ordinary things, such as pieces of wood, polished stones, plants or animals, are sacred objects once they bear the emblem of the totem. The totemic object gives the clan its name and identity. Many taboos are attached to the totemic object which cannot be killed or eaten, and it must be treated with respect. The totemic objects are well connected with the clan. The clan is not necessarily related by blood, but they have a common name and emblem. In this way, religion and society are connected in simple societies.

The totem, according to Durkheim, represents a group in three crucial respects. First, it means the group's collective beliefs and social practices to the individuals who make it up. Second, it represents the collective to itself historically in its legends and myths. Third, it means the collective to itself in the form of total social reality (Durkheim, 1965: 119). The totem may thus be described as an institution that leads to three distinct kinds of religious activity: first is a system of beliefs and rites that unify and bind the social group together around a sacred object. Second, is a system of interdictions that sets out what individual obligations are toward this sacred object. Third, totemism is a system of rites for worshipping sacred things (Morrison, 1995: 195).

Durkheim maintains that it is not the animal or plants themselves that is worshipped or held sacred, but an unknown and impersonal force that exists throughout the world and is diffused amongst all the material objects of the world. Thus, the totems are the material representations of the immaterial force at their base. Moreover, that immaterial force is none other than the collective conscience of society. Durkheim stated,

> Totemism is the religion, not of such and such animals or men or images, but of an anonymous and impersonal force found in each of

these beings without being identified with any one of them. None possess it entirely, and all participate in it. So independent is it of the particular subjects in which it is embodied that it precedes them just as it is adequate. Individuals die; generations pass away and are replaced by others. But this force remains over the present, living, and true to itself. It quickens today's generation just as it quickens yesterday's and as it will quicken tomorrow. (1965: 217)

Totemism and religion are derived from collective morality and become an impersonal force. It is not simply a series of mythical animals, plants, personalities, spirits, or gods. The essence of totemism, according to Durkheim, is the worship of an impersonal, anonymous force, at once immanent and transcendent. This unknown diffuse force, superior to men and very close to them is, in reality, society itself.

In short, totemism is a symbolic representation of the collective conscience, and the collective conscience, in turn, is derived from society. Therefore, society is the source of collective conscience, religion, and ultimately, the concept of God. Durkheim argued that God and society are the same in an absolute sense. It remains true even today. If religion is nothing but the indirect worship of society, modern people only need to express their religious feelings directed toward the sacred symbolization of society. In this context, society's worship strengthens the values and moral beliefs that form the basis of social life. In worshipping society, men are in effect, recognizing the importance of the social group and their dependence upon it. In this way, religion strengthens the unity of the group. It promotes social solidarity.

V. INDIVIDUAL AND SOCIETY

Human beings, according to Durkheim, are creatures with unlimited desires. However, unlike other animals, they are not satisfied until and unless their biological needs are fulfilled. 'The more one has, the more one wants since satisfactions received only stimulate instead of filling needs' (Durkheim, 1951: 248). Human desire can only be checked by external or societal control. Society imposes limits on human desires and constitutes 'a regulative force (which) must play the same role for moral needs which the organism plays for physical needs' (ibid.). Society constitutes a regulative force that sets certain limits on individual passions.

When social regulations breakdown, the controlling mechanism of society on the individual is no longer effective, and individuals are left to their wishes. Durkheim calls this state of affairs as *anomie* or *normlessness*. It characterizes a condition in which standard norms no longer regulate individual desires, leaving individuals without moral guidelines for pursuing their goals.

The preceding discussion on the individual and society in Durkheim's sociology explains the forces contributing to social regulation and deregulation. It mainly depends on a particular person's situation in a specific society. Any rapid movement in the social structure that upsets previous networks in which lifestyles are embedded carries a chance of anomie. By stimulating human desires, Durkheim argued that economic affluence carries with it the dangers of anomic conditions because it 'deceives us into believing that we depend on ourselves only'. At the same time, 'poverty protects against suicide because it is a restraint in itself' (Durkheim, 1951: 254). Durkheim's programme of study, according to Lewis Coser, is mainly concerned with the problems of social order and disorder (Coser, 1996: 113). He addresses the tensions between individual desires and social cohesion and balances individual and societal claims.

The relationship between the individual and society is complex, according to Durkheim. In *The Division of Labour in Society*, Durkheim discusses two types of societies based on mechanical and organic solidarity. Mechanical solidarity is mainly concerned with the individual's 'collective conscience', whereas the increasing level of individualism marks organic solidarity. Durkheim talks in favour of organic solidarity because he sees it as a state where individual concerns can help build stronger societal bonds.

Durkheim probably saw society as a special kind of organism. He claimed that society has its existence as *sui-generis*. Society has existed in its own right as a separate independent entity. It existed before the individual and will continue to exist long after individuals. Its members are born and die, but society lives on. Individuals cannot exist without or apart from society. Hence, this view of society gives a picture of Durkheim's understanding of the relationship between individuals and society.

VI. FUNCTIONALISM

In the writings of Emile Durkheim, the concept of function took on a greater methodological significance, and he is widely regarded as a functionalist by sociologists and social anthropologists. Functionalism, for Durkheim, was his alternative to both Comte's and Spencer's teleological methods. Much of Durkheim's work is concerned with functional analysis, seeking to understand the functions of social facts. He believes that society has specific functional prerequisites. Moreover, these functional prerequisites play a crucial role in the maintenance of 'social order'. Thus, the functional analysis aims to clarify how institutions and other social phenomena contribute to maintaining the social whole.

Durkheim established the functional approach to society by establishing a clear distinction between historical and functional types of enquiries and between functional consequences and individual motivations. 'The determination of function', says Durkheim, 'is necessary for the complete explanation of the phenomena. To explain a social fact is not enough to show the cause on which it depends; we must also show its function in the establishment of social order' (Durkheim, 1938: 103).

On the other hand, Haralambos (1999: 524-6) sees Durkheim's position on functional analysis in his concept of 'collective conscience'. The collective conscience constrains individuals to act in terms of the requirements of society. Since the collective conscience is a social fact and therefore external to the individual, it must be imposed upon him.

Durkheim's functionalism may be illustrated in the theory of religion.

> Social order requires that individuals experience society within themselves, realize their dependence upon it and recognize their fundamentally social obligations. By symbolizing society and making it sacred, religion meets these requirements. It makes social life possible by expressing, maintaining and reinforcing the sentiments or values which form the collective conscience. Social obligations are represented in sacred terms and so transformed into religious duties.... In symbolizing society, religion awakens in the individual an appreciation of his reliance on society. By recognizing his dependence on society, religion integrates the social group since those who share religious beliefs' feel united by the simple fact that they have a common faith'. The highly charged atmosphere of religious rituals dramatizes this unity and promotes social solidarity. In this way, religion functions to meet the essential requirements of social life. (Haralambos, 1999: 526)

VII. CONCLUSION

Durkheim is one of the classical theorists in social sciences in general and sociology in particular. He is best known as the founding fathers of sociology as a scientific discipline and defines its subject matter's boundaries. Durkheim contributes to sociological concepts, perspectives, approaches, methods, and theories. He belongs to the functional school of thought. In this context, he tries to establish a distinct discipline of society, called sociology. Here, his primary concern was to discuss the issue of social solidarity or integration of society. He mainly emphasizes the notion of *sui-generis*. Durkheim is concerned with discussing society as a whole and the rise of individualism. However, his method of explaining and characterizing social order, as Durkheim discussed it, is mainly focused on the consensus model of society.

Durkheim's sociology is considered as most scientific in his explanation by contemporary sociologists. He discussed the nature and scope of sociology in the methodological part of his writings. The rule of the sociological method is a programmatic statement about the causes of sociology as a discipline, with its specific subject matter and methodology. In this sense, he deals with the concept of *social facts* that are 'external to the individual'. Durkheim, here proposed that sociological analysis must be done with macro-level causal-functional analysis. However, he defines sociology as 'the science of institutions, their genesis, and functioning'. Durkheim has applied his methodological orientation of *social facts* and the notion of *sui-generis* throughout his sociological writings.

Durkheim, throughout his writings, tries to establish relationships between society and the individual. However, his central theme is the priority of society over the individual. This fact can be seen in his major writings, *The Division of Labour in Society*, *Suicide* and *The Elementary Forms of Religious Life*. In these writings, Durkheim emphasized the concept of *collective conscience*. Durkheim describes collective conscience as 'the body of beliefs and sentiments common to the average members of a society'. In the division of labour in society, Durkheim makes a fruitful attempt to analyse different types of society in terms of traditional or tribal society (mechanical solidarity) and modern society (organic solidarity) in an evolutionary way. In *Suicide*, he tries to find out the causes of suicide in the social roots rather than individual or psychological phenomena. The latter part of his work, the sociology of religion, emphasizes social cohesion. In the sociology of religion, he discovers the roots of religious activities in the concept of *Totemism*, a 'primitive and most simple form of religion' of the Arunta tribes of the Australian aboriginal.

Durkheim will always be remembered for his contribution to sociology as a distinct discipline. Durkheim, however, was not free from criticism. He has mainly been criticized for giving more emphasis on collectivity. He only emphasized on well-integrated society. In this way, he could not see the social function of conflict. As we know, conflict is found in every type of society, whether primitive or modern. The difference is found only in the nature and frequency of the conflict. He therefore, was criticized for not making any contribution to social conflict. In addition to it, he could not adequately stress the role of differences of dissent in human society. Despite various criticisms, he is still acknowledged as a pioneer and outstanding sociologist.

KEY TERMS

Agelicism: The sociological position, represented by Emile Durkheim, maintains that social phenomena have an independent reality and cannot be reduced to or explained in merely individual terms. The social group is seen as more than a sum of the individuals who comprise it.

Altruism: The state of society or a social group in which the individual is completely merged with the group and has no interests apart from those of the group.

Animatism: The belief that a supernatural force or power exists in persons, animals, and inanimate objects. Robert R. Merrett introduced the concept in his book *The Threshold of Religion*.

Animism: The belief that all objects, both animate and inanimate, are permanently or temporarily inhabited by spirits or souls. Edward B. Tylor maintained that animism was man's earliest form of religion in his book *Primitive Culture*.

Anomie: A condition characterized by the relative absence or confusion of values in a society or group. As initially developed by Emile Durkheim, 'this concept referred to a property of the social and cultural structure, not to a property of individuals confronting that structure'.

Belief: A statement about reality that is partially based on faith.

Clan: A unilateral kin group based on either matrilineal or patrilineal descent.

Cohesion, social: The integration of group behaviour due to social bonds, attractions, or 'forces' that hold members of a group in interaction over time.

Collective conscience: According to Durkheim, collective conscience refers to the totality of beliefs and sentiments common to an average member of society.

Collective effervescence: A collective feeling of enthusiasm and excitement that strengthens bonds between individuals and members feel proud for belonging to that society. Durkheim has used this term.

Collective representation: A term introduced by Emile Durkheim to express collective sentiments and ideas, which give the group unity and unique character.

Consensus: Agreement amongst the members of society regarding social norms, values, allocation of roles and rewards. Consensus helps to maintain social order.

Custom: It refers to the established mode of behaviour, thought, and action practised and transferred from generation to generation.

Division of labour: A functionally integrated system of occupational roles or specializations within a society.

Division of labour, anomic: One of the significant abnormal forms of the division of labour distinguished by Emile Durkheim. The anomic division of labour occurs when extreme specialization is accompanied by a decline in communication between persons performing different functions.

Forced division of labour: One of the significant abnormal forms of the division of labour distinguished by Emile Durkheim. The forced division of labour occurs when individuals are compelled to take on occupational roles that they do not like and are not suited to.

Functional model of society: This is the way of looking at a society that stresses social order and studies how different social institutions and subsystems function or maintain social order.

Horde: Small band of people related through kinship ties. They are found among nomadic hunters and food gatherers.

Lineage: A group of kin who traces descent from a known common ancestor, conducted in a single line, either only through patrilineal or only matrilineal.

Naturism: The philosophical doctrine that all phenomena, whether physical, mental, or social, are determined by and explainable in terms of the law of nature.

Norm: A specific guide to action defines an appropriate and acceptable behaviour in a particular situation.

Normlessness: A condition characterized by the absence of an organized system of social norms of values that enable an individual to choose the most desirable action in a situation.

Polysegmental: It describes more than one segment.

Positivist: It is based on practical experience. The term *positivism* denotes the scientific model on which early sociology developed it.

Profane: The elements of a social system not connected with religion or religious purposes.

Repressive law: Law that punishes the wrong doer for establishing the power and authority of the group or the collectivity. The most prevalent type of law was practised in primitive societies.

Restitutive law: Restitutive law is the characteristic of modern society where everything is guided based on prescribed rules and regulations.

Sacred: The sacred is often associated with religion and is sometimes considered synonymous with the holy.

Social solidarity: That condition within a group with social cohesion plus cooperative, collective action directed toward achieving group goals.

Sui-generis: It generates itself and exists by itself. It does not depend upon some other being for its origin or existence—Durkheim considered society *sui-generis*. It is always present and has no point of origin.

Suicide: Death results from deliberate self-destruction or inaction when it is known that inaction will have fatal consequences.

Suicide, altruistic: A type of suicide in which an individual closely integrates into a group or society kills himself for the group's welfare.

Suicide, anomic: A type of suicide resulting from normlessness or social and personal disorganization.

Suicide, egoistic: Suicide is due to strong social norms for which the individual feels personally responsible, resulting in an overwhelming burden on the individual.

Taboo: A strong social norm prohibiting specific actions that the group or community punishable, supernatural, or magical consequences.

Totem: A class of objects, usually a species of animal, a type of plant or inanimate thing that is regarded by a clan, lineage, other social groups as having a special relationship to the social unit. Totem is treated as religious which cannot be harmed or destroyed.

Totemism: Durkheim suggested that totemism was an early and elementary form of religion that provided a collective religious object which was a decisive factor in developing social cohesion within early society.

REFERENCES

Abraham, Francis and J.H. Morgan, *Sociological Thought,* Macmillan India, Chennai, 1985.

Aron, Raymond, *Main Currents in Sociological Thought* (II), Doubleday, Garden City, 1970.

Coser, Lewis A., *Masters of Sociological Thought,* Rawat Publications, Jaipur and New Delhi, 1996.

Craib, Ian, *Classical Social Theory: An Introduction to the Thought of Marx, Weber, Durkheim, and Simmel,* Oxford University Press, New York, 1997.

Cuff, E.C., W.W. Sharrock and D.W. Francis, *Perspectives in Sociology,* Unwin Hyman, London, 1990.

Durkheim, E., *Suicide,* Free Press, New York, (1897) 1951.

——, *The Division of Labour in Society,* The Free Press, Glencoe: New York, 1964.

——, *The Elementary Forms of Religious Life,* Free Press, New York, (1912) 1965.

——, *The Rules of Sociological Method*, Free Press, New York, (1895) 1938.

Haralambos, M. and R.M. Heald, *Sociology: Themes and Perspectives*, Oxford University Press, New Delhi, 1999.

Lukes, S., *Emile Durkheim: His Life and Work*, Stanford University Press, Stanford, 1973.

Morrison, Ken, *Marx, Durkheim, Weber: Formation of Modern Social Thought*, Sage Publications, London, 1995.

Pope, Whitney, *Durkheim's Suicide: A Classic Analysed*, University of Chicago Press, Chicago, USA, 1976.

Rex, John, *Key Problems in Sociological Theory*, Routledge and Kegan Paul, London, 1961.

Ritzer, George, *Sociological Theory*, McGraw-Hill Publishing Company, Singapore, 1988.

CHAPTER 5

Max Weber
1864-1920

BIOGRAPHICAL SKETCH

Max Weber is considered one of the central figures of social science in general and sociological theory in particular. Max Weber was born in Erfurt, Germany, into a middle-class protestant family on 21 April 1864. His father was a well-known politician who played a minor role in his upbringing. However, Weber's mother had a significant contribution throughout his life. At the age of eighteen, he left home for a short time to attend the University of Heidelberg. However, he left Heidelberg for military service, and in 1884 he returned to Berlin and to his parent's home to take courses at the University of Berlin. At the University of Berlin, he obtained a university degree in law and eventually a doctorate in political economy. In 1894, Weber joined Freiburg University as a professor of Political Economy. In 1897, he joined Heidelberg University as a professor of Economics. He was considered very young to obtain a significant German university professorship at thirty-two. However, the following year, a severe personal crisis forced Weber to suspend his teaching activities and eventually resign his position at Heidelberg (Weber, Marianne, 1975). But in 1897, his father died. Shortly after that, a severe nervous breakdown occurred in his life, from which he never fully recovered. After his recovery, he became an Honorary Professor at Heidelberg University in 1903, where he began to return to his active academic life.

After that, he began to return to regular intellectual work in 1904. Weber published his most famous work, *The Protestant*

Max Weber (1864-1920)

Ethic and the Spirit of Capitalism, between 1904 and 1905 based on the relationship between capitalism and religion. By 1909, Weber began writing *Economy and Society*, his most ambitious, theoretical and historical work. During 1916-17, he researched the history of world religions (China, India, and ancient Judaism). His last academic work was a series of lectures that he gave at the University of Freiburg in 1919-20, entitled *General Economic History* based on the history of capitalist development.

In addition to the significant writings produced in this period, Weber undertook several other activities. German Sociological Society was established in 1910 with the help of Weber. As a result, his home became a centre for many intellectuals, including sociologists such as George Simmel, Robert Michaels, and Georg Lukacs. Weber was also active in politics and wrote essays on the issue of the day (Weber, Marianne, 1975: 65). Weber died in June 1920.

Weber's intellectual works are considered best for their historical explanation of modern Western societies and their economic, political, legal, and religious development. Weber's significant contributions to social sciences are methodological orientation, analysis of social class, theory of legitimacy and religion, etc. In addition, he focused on the issues of the rise of modern society, the formation of bureaucracy, the development of the modern political state and comparative world economics (Tribe, 1989). Weber was a modernist and individualistic in his approach. He brought together various traditions of social thought and formed a unique theoretical perspective based on history, economics, philosophy, law and comparative historical analysis. Weber, in reality, was influenced by the Marxist school of economics and opposed on several fronts, which led him to formulate a completely different view of the role played by history and economy in social development.

I. WEBER'S METHODOLOGY

Weber's methodology is primarily related to *Methodenstreit* or the German debate about the proper method for the social sciences. However, Weber wanted social science to seek causal arguments that would generalize social actions and pay attention to the context in which an action occurs. In this sense, 'Max Weber conceived of sociology as a comprehensive science of social action' (Aron, 1967: 181). To comprehend the meaning of social action, Weber prescribed the application of two essential and interrelated methods: (i) *Verstehen* (understanding), and (ii) Ideal types construction.

Weber's methodological works appear in his two writings. First is *Roscher and Knies: The Logical Problems of Historical Economics*, written between 1902 and 1903. A second work called 'Objectivity in Social Science and Social Policy' was written between 1903 and 1904 (Weber, 1975, 1949). Thus, to understand Weber's methodology, we must look at some of the methodological issues that developed between 1880 and 1900. In this context, the methodological views of two Neo-Kantian thinkers, Wilhelm Windelb and and Heinrich Rickert have to be discussed.

Windelband focuses on method and argues that the scientific disciplines are distinct from the social and historical sciences. It is because of their different methodologies rather than their different subject matters. He reasoned that two kinds of methodological approaches are distinct. First, natural sciences aim to produce general laws and explain events by observation and deductive methods about the physical world's structure. This leads to the scientific generalizing tendency that confirms reality (Wiley, 1978: 154). The aim is to focus on individual events to determine their formative characteristics by deriving a picture of what took place. In this case, the historical sciences must adopt inductive methods, i.e. methods based on observation and information gathered about an event. Windelband thought that the natural sciences are thus *nomothetic* or law-giving in their methods and orientations, making them general in how they treat reality (Beck, 1967: 470). The historical sciences or social sciences, by contrast, are *ideographic* in their orientation, i.e., they assemble information about events to arrive at a picture of the whole. In this way, Windelband argues that either of these approaches could study any given object, and he takes the position that an accurate picture of the world could be obtained using both kinds of methods (Morrison, 1995: 259).

On the other hand, Rickert distinguishes between the natural and social sciences based on method and methodological approach. He believes that the natural sciences deal with types of subject matter whose events are recurring in nature and can be captured by laws. But the historical sciences, by contrast, tend to explain what he calls 'individual non-recurring events' (Anchor, 2013: 192-4). Thus, Rickert views that the natural sciences demonstrate the empirical world by *generalizing* methodology compared to the *individualizing* method of the historical sciences. In addition, human beings are value-conferring by nature, but on the other hand, Rickert argues, the products of nature are devoid of values. 'The presence or absence of values', Rickert reasoned, 'thus must serve as a reliable criterion for distinguishing between two kinds of scientific objects and two kinds of science' (Rickert, 1962: 18-19). The first set of objects belong to the natural world, and these exist independent of human agency. The second set is the social and cultural objects directly produced by human agents concerning valued ends.

VALUE-RELEVANCE

To understand Weber's methodological orientation of *Verstehen* and Ideal types construction, it is necessary to look at the notion of 'value' in natural and social sciences. Rickert uses the concept of Value Relevance. Rickert considers that the principle of value relevance can only apply when scientists use concepts. Without concept formation there is no understanding: thus concepts separate the essential from the inessential. Hence, the historical sciences depend on empirical reality selection to arrive at their subject matter (Morrison, 1995: 269). Thus, the historian selects material using a value relation. The value relation refers to the idea that a particular phenomenon is 'worthy of interest' based on the scheme of value current in society (Bruun, 1972: 88-9). In reaction to this, Weber believed that the subject matter of the social sciences was made up of individuals whose social action was based on values. This led Weber to assert that the social sciences must begin understanding how these values act as a basis of social action. Therefore, Weber showed that the social sciences must arrive at a methodology encompassing both general and individual aspects of historical reality (Morrison, 1995: 267). Hence, for Weber, values are central to the subject matter of his methods and applied to the scientific study of human actions. He is the leading spokesman for *the value-free approach in sociology*. In his/her study of society, the sociologist or researcher is primarily concerned with analysing and understanding values. Therefore, sociologists must not let one's values come in the way of a clear understanding of the subject matter. In this sense, a value-free social science development is necessary for creating a body of reliable and assured knowledge.

The entire debate of value relevance of Weberian thought, Shills and Finch summarized it in the following words:

> The scientific treatment of value judgements may understand and empathetically analyse the desired ends and the ideals that underline them and 'judge' them critically. This criticism can . . . be no more than a formal logical judgement of historically given value judgements and ideas, a testing of the ideals according to the postulate of the internal *consistency* of the desired end. It can assist (the acting person) in becoming aware of the ultimate standards of value which he does not make explicit to himself, or which he must presuppose in order to be logical. As to whether the person expressing these value judgements *should* adhere to these ultimate standards in his personal affair; it involves will and conscience, not empirical knowledge. (1949: 54)

Nevertheless, the other face of reality is that the personal involvement of the investigator can hardly avoid his values and interests in a particular situation. Therefore, the choice of the problem is always 'value relevant'. In this context, Weber argues:

> There is no absolutely 'objective' scientific analysis of a culture or . . . of 'social phenomena' independent of special and 'one-sided' viewpoints according to which . . . expressly or tacitly, consciously or unconsciously . . . they are selected, analysed and organized for expository purposes. (Shills & Finch, 1949: 72)

Therefore, what is considered 'worthy of being known' depends upon the perspective and understanding of the investigator.

Value relevance should be distinguished from value-neutrality because they refer to two different orders of ideas. Value relevance is that ethical neutrality which implies that once the social scientist has chosen his problem regarding its significance to his values, he must hold values—his own or others. He can not impose his values on the data, and he is compelled to pursue his line of inquiry. On the other, value-neutrality refers to the normative function that the ethos of science should govern men of science in their role as scientists. In other words, value-neutrality refers to the disjunction between the world of facts and the world of values (Coser, 1996: 221-2).

In addition, Aron distinguished between value judgement (*Werturteil*) and value reference (*Wertbeziehung*) to tackle the challenge of developing a universalized value judgement using socio-historical instances of human creativity. According to Aron, judgements are personal and necessarily subjective, dependent upon one's values and beliefs. On the other, the term *value reference* means that the sociologist of politics will regard freedom of expression as a matter on which historical subjects have disagreed. Thus, he can explore the past or present political reality by emphasizing the specific value, 'freedom'. Therefore, to be true to the method of Weber, value relevance must be thought of as bearing upon the 'selection of problem' but not upon 'the interpretation of the phenomenon' (Abraham & Morgan, 1985: 109).

Therefore, it can be said that values are a primary device for selecting subjects to study and a necessity for acquiring meaningful knowledge of the social world. Thus, values play a crucial role before, during, and after social research.

VERSTEHEN

Verstehen is one of the key concepts or approaches of Weber's methodology. It is a German word that means 'understanding'. The *Versteben* is based on the idea that meaning precedes action. We cannot act unless we know the importance of other acts. Weber thought this meaning constituted a positive basis for distinguishing between the natural and social sciences. Weber used the term *verstehen* in the context of a theory of social action.

Weber believes that sociologists have an advantage over natural scientists. We can only observe uniformities in the natural sciences and deduce generalizations about the natural world and the other states. By contrast, the social sciences are subjective, where the 'inner states' of actors act on their 'understanding' (*Verstehen*) of the acts of others and their interpretation of the social environment. Therefore, the advantage resided in the sociologist's ability to understand social phenomena. Dilthey's philosophical perspective is related to Weber's method in this context. Coser stated,

> Dilthey opposed positivism by constructing the outlines of an approach to the data of human culture and human history, which, though meant to be scientific, was wholly at variance with the approach of the natural sciences. Knowledge of man's world, Dilthey claimed, could only be attained through an internal process, through experience (*Erlbaum*) and understanding (*Verstehen*) rather than through merely external knowledge. . . . The natural sciences (*Naturwissenschaften*) can do no more than explain (*eklaeren*) observed events by relating them to natural laws. In the humanistic disciplines, the *Geistewissenschaften*, knowledge is not external but internal. Men are intelligible to us in their uniqueness and individuality (Coser, 1996: 245).

Through this passage, we can say that Weber's methodological concept of *Verstehen* is based on the individual's experience in a social situation. Hence, the Weberian approach is related to natural scientists understanding the natural phenomena from outside the problem. In contrast, social scientists understand social phenomena through participation in the situation.

In addition, Rossides explains, 'for Weber, *Versteben* sociology was not a search for the underlying principle of existence, but a conscious search for insights and solutions to the unique and changing problems that human beings face, all orientation that Weber stated epigrammatically when he said that social science has 'external youth' (1978: 377).

Weber's unique use of *Verstehen* in his historical research is one of his best-known contributions to the methodology of contemporary sociology. Weber's thought on *Verstehen* was relatively common among German historians of his day and was derived from a field known as *hermeneutics* (Mueller-Vollmer, 1985: 1-53). *Hermeneutics* was a unique approach to the understanding and interpretation of published works. Its goal was to understand the author's ideas and the basic theme of his work. Furthermore, Weber sought to extend this idea from understanding texts to the knowledge of social life. In other words, Weber sought to use the tools of hermeneutics to understand actors, interactions, and indeed all of human history. *Hermeneutics* has become a major intellectual concern in recent years, especially in the work of Martin Heidegger, Hans-Georg Gadamer, and Jürgen Habermas (Bleicher, 1980). In brief, according to Weber, *Verstehen* involved systematic and rigorous research rather than simply getting a 'feeling' for a text or social phenomenon. In other words, for Weber, *Verstehen* was a rational procedure of the study (Weber, 1968).

CAUSALITY AND PROBABILITY

Weber's methodology is concerned with placing the concept of values in social sciences and understanding the notion of *Verstehen* in the field of natural and social sciences and involve the study of the causes and probability of social phenomena. Causality and probability are the dominant aspects of Weber's methodology. Weber was interested in understanding the causes of social phenomena within history, not sociology.

By *Causality*, Weber meant the probability that an event will be followed or accompanied by another event. Weber made a distinction between historical causality and sociological causality for causal inquiry.

> Historical causality determines the unique circumstances that have given rise to a given event. Sociological causality assumes the establishment of a stable relationship between two phenomena, which need not take the form 'A makes B inevitable', but may take the form 'A is more or less favorable to B'. (Aron, 1970: 193)

Weber's understanding of historical causality has its roots in past events, whereas sociological causality discusses the present relationship between two phenomena.

In addition, Weber also talked about *multiple causalities* in his study of the relationship between Protestantism and the spirit of capitalism. For example, Weber argued that the protestant ethic was one of the causal factors in the rise of the modern spirit of capitalism. In other words, capitalism could have arisen due to the Protestant Reformation, but other factors could have led to the same result. Weber pointed out:

> As far as possible, we shall clarify the manner and the general *direction* in which . . . the religious movements have influenced the development of material culture. Only when this has been determined with reasonable accuracy can the attempt be made to estimate the historical development of modern culture be attributed to those *religious forces* and to *what extent to others*. (1958: 91-2)

Weber had a primary interest in causality in all his historical works. Weber's thinking on causality mainly represents his belief in understanding social life (*Verstehen*) and distinguishing between the causal knowledge of social sciences and natural sciences. As Weber puts it,

> Meaningfully interpretable human conduct (action) is identifiable by reference to 'valuation' and meanings. For this reason, our criteria for *causal* explanation have a unique kind of satisfaction in the 'historical' explanation of such an 'entity'. (Weber, 1975: 185)

Thus, the causal knowledge of the social scientist is different from and 'better than' the causal knowledge of the natural scientist.

Weber's thought on causality is also related to nomothetic and idiographic knowledge. Those who subscribe to a nomothetic perspective would argue a necessary relationship among social phenomena. In contrast, the supporters of an idiographic viewpoint would be inclined to see the only random relationship among these entities. In this situation, Weber took a middle position and described the concept of objective possibility (Frank, 1976: 18). The notion of *objective possibility* adopts the view that the best we can do in sociology is to make probabilistic statements about the relationship between social phenomena. 'If x occurs, then it is *probable* that I will occur. The goal is to "estimate" the degree to which a particular effect is "favoured" by certain "conditions"' (Weber, 1949: 183).

IDEAL TYPES

Weber first put forth the ideal type in 'objectivity in social science and social policy', which he published in 1905. The ideal type is the best-known contribution of Weber to contemporary sociology. An ideal type is a conceptual and methodological tool to study a particular social situation or problem. He developed ideal types for making scientific generalizations out of our understanding of this infinitely complex and shifting world. According to Coser (1996: 223), 'An ideal type is an analytical construct that serves the investigator as a measuring rod to ascertain similarities as well as deviations in concrete cases. It provides the basic method for comparative study.' Therefore, an ideal type is selecting certain elements, traits, or characteristics that are distinctive and relevant to the phenomenon under study.

> An ideal type is formed by the one-sided accentuation of one or more points of view and by the synthesis of a great many diffuse, discrete, more or less present and occasionally absent *concrete individual* phenomena, which are arranged according to those one-sidedly emphasized viewpoints into a unified analytical construct. . . . This mental construct . . . cannot be found empirically anywhere in reality in its conceptual purity. (Weber, 1949: 90)

Despite this definition, Weber was not consistent in dealing with the ideal type. In this sense, an ideal type never corresponds to a concrete reality but always moves at least one step away. In Weber's view, 'the ideal type was derived inductively from the real world of social history. But Weber did not believe that it was enough to offer a careful analysis of concepts, especially if they were deductively derived from an abstract theory' (Ritzer, 1988: 107). Thus, it can be said that an ideal is a mental construction formed by exaggerating certain essential features of a given phenomenon. In brief, ideal types are heuristic devices valuable and helpful to conducting empirical research and making us understand the social world. In this sense, Weber stated: 'The ideal typical concept will develop our skill in imputation in research. It is not a description of reality, but it aims to give unambiguous means of expression to such a description' (Weber, 1972: 63).

In other words, ideal types are concepts formulated based on facts collected carefully and analysed for empirical research. Hence, ideal types are constructs or concepts used as methodological devices or tools to understand and analyse any social problem or social situation.

CHARACTERISTICS OF IDEAL TYPES

Based on the above discussion, we can draw some essential characteristics of ideal types. These are:

(i) The ideal types are subjective. It is based on the notion of *Verstehen* (understanding) and *value relevance*. At the same time, he also emphasizes causal knowledge. According to him, the causal knowledge of the social scientist is both different from and 'better than' the causal knowledge of the natural scientist. However, causal knowledge leads to subjectivity in the construction of ideal types.

(ii) The ideal types are the mental construction of any individual, and therefore it depends on particular time and space. When change takes place, the ideal type will also be changed. Therefore, ideal types are considered to be changeable.

(iii) Ideal types are neither the presentation of total reality nor the explanation of everything. Thus, 'Weber never claimed the ideal type to exhaust every conceivable empirical structure completely (Abraham & Morgan, 1985: 177).

(iv) Ideal types are not a description of any definite concept of reality or a hypothesis; they provide only a definition and explanation of a particular situation based on the mental construct. 'It is neither a statistical average nor hypothesis; rather it is a mental construct, an organization of intelligible relations within a historical entity, formed by exaggerating certain essential features of a given phenomenon that falls within the definitional framework' (Abraham & Morgan, 1985: 176). In this sense, ideal types are not general or average types. Instead, they are formulated based on certain typical traits essential to constructing an ideal type concept.

(v) An ideal type is an analytical construct that provides the primary method for comparative study.

(vi) An ideal type has nothing to do with a moral ideal. Any social phenomenon has an ideal type: a brothel, a house of worship, or a marketplace.

Ideal types cover a wide range of content and subject matter. Ideal types serve to guide empirical research. In this context, Weber explains:

> Whatever be the content of the ideal type, be it an ethical, a legal, aesthetic, or a religious form, or a technical, economic, or cultural maxim or any other type of valuation in the most rational form possible, it has only one function in an empirical investigation. Its function is the compare with empirical reality to establish its divergences or similarities, describe them with the most unambiguously intelligible concepts, and understand and explain them causally. (Abraham & Morgan, 1985: 177)

In this regard, we assume that ideal types are also related to the analytic conception of causality.

IDEAL TYPES IN WEBER'S WORK

Weber used three kinds of ideal types based on their levels of abstraction (Coser, 1996: 224). The first ideal type is rooted in historical particularities, such as the 'Western city', 'the protestant ethic', or 'modern capitalism'. This ideal type refers to phenomena that appear only in specific historical periods and cultural areas. The second kind of ideal type refers to abstract elements of social reality, for example, the concepts of bureaucracy or feudalism. These elements of social reality are observable in various historical and cultural contexts. The third ideal type relates to the 'rationalising reconstructions of a particular kind of behaviour' (Aron, 1967: 204).

The first ideal type is the main category of type formation based on historical particulars. Hence, it can also be called historical ideal type formation. Historical ideal types form concepts by selecting phenomena based on common characteristics and employ the criterion of selection of only those general concepts 'precisely and unambiguously definable, such as individualism, feudalism, and capitalism' (Weber, 1949: 50-112). In this sense, the ideal type is designed to capture features of empirical reality by arriving at what Weber referred to as the 'analytical accentuation' of certain aspects of social-historical reality (Morrison, 1995: 270-1). For instance, the ideal type construction of 'city economy' is necessary to outline the 'city economy' essential traits. The basic traits of a city economy may include such elements as a system of law based on statutes, a decline of magic, and a system of private property. Other traits related to a city economy may include the concept of a citizen, a municipal organization, and a bureaucracy created by political office-holders (Weber, 1961: 238).

The second ideal type refers to abstract elements of the historical reality observable in various historical and cultural contexts. An example of this type of construction can be found in Weber's comparison of the shift from a system of administration by notables to a modern system of bureaucratic administration. This type is constructed by forming the general concept of administration by notables and isolating common elements such as their means of legitimacy, type of administration, degree of calculation in decisions, and the characteristics of a law system. The 'shift' from such a system to a modern bureaucratic administration may be conditioned by specific factors such as a system of legal authority, the dominance of formal rationality, a hierarchy of offices and decision-makers, and reliance upon written documentation and record-keeping (Weber, 1949: 101). Weber used these abstract elements of bureaucracy to explain a concrete phenomenon. In addition to bureaucracy, Weber also constructed ideal types of authority and social action.

The third ideal type relates to reconstructing a particular type of behaviour. For example, all propositions in economic theory are considered to be this type of ideal type construction. The economic theory deals with the laws of supply and demand, marginal utilities, etc. The supply of the commodity in the market governs prices concerning demand. Similarly, the utility of a commodity for consumption is higher or lower depends on the units available for consumption. Economic theory rigorously conceives economic behaviour as consistent with its essence (Weber, 1964: 210).

PURPOSE AND USE OF IDEAL TYPES

The purpose and use of ideal types are mainly based on their construction rather than describing historical types. It all happens based on the present knowledge of the investigator (Weber, 1949: 101). The primary purpose of the ideal type is to make explicit both the general and individual characteristics of empirical reality. Weber is reliant on Windelband's nomothetic-ideographic distinction and the generalizing-individualizing distinction of Rickert. The nomothetic sciences, i.e. natural sciences, aim at constructing general laws and explaining individual events by identifying events.

In contrast, the ideographic sciences, i.e. historical sciences, look at the individual event to arrive at a general pattern. Rickert stated that the natural sciences explain the empirical world by what he called a 'generalizing' methodology in contrast to the 'individualizing' methodology of the historical sciences. Under these circumstances, the goal of the ideal type are to 'frame out' the empirical characteristics of reality. Weber, like Rickert, knew that empirical reality could not be described in any complete factual sense, but he did believe it could be 'framed out' using criteria of selection (Morrison, 1995: 272-3). Therefore, ideal types are constructed to facilitate the analysis of empirical questions.

According to Weber,

> the ideal type serves several distinct investigative purposes. First, it can discover relationships of the types referred to in concrete reality by seeing if they exist and whether their characteristics can be clear and understandable. Second, it is indispensable for heuristic and expository purposes since it helps understand the kinds of activities assigned to different societies during research. Third, while it is not a hypothesis, it offers constructive help in forming hypotheses. Fourth, while an ideal type is not a description of reality, it can reduce ambiguity about empirical reality by providing the means to foster adequate descriptions of it. Fifth, the ideal type leads to the formation of concepts about societies by holding ideas of historically given types of societies within its conceptual understanding of reality. (Morrison, 1995: 273)

In brief, the ideal type is a methodological procedure used to discover common properties of social phenomena. Thus, the ideal type is designed to capture empirical reality by arriving at the 'analytical accentuation' of certain aspects of society. The main category of ideal type construction, according to Weber, is the ideal historical type.

II. WEBER'S THEORY OF SOCIAL ACTION

Max Weber perceived sociology as a comprehensive science of social action. Weber's theory of social action is related to his methodological approach. Weber first developed the theory of social action in *Economy and Society*, which he wrote between 1911 and 1920. Weber's theory of social action eventually embraced 'meaningful' social action and attempted to incorporate the relevance of values in a theory of human action. Weber's theory of action is the product of the *Methodenstreit.*

In the background of this theory, Weber made two fundamental points: firstly, sociology must concern itself with interpreting social action; secondly, it must devise a social theory of values. Weber's social action theory may be defined as the body of social theory he developed to make valid judgements about actors' 'inner states' in their actions. By 'inner states', Weber refers to the actor's capacity to choose between the means and ends of action and exercise 'rational' choice (Morrison, 1995: 274). Weber's theory of social action involves four central concepts: (i) the concept of understanding or *Verstehen;* (ii) the concept of 'interpretive understanding' (iii) the concept of subjective meaning; and (iv) the concept of social action.Thus, the central theme of the theory of social action is:

> Sociology is a science that attempts the interpretive understanding of social action to arrive at a causal explanation of its course and effects. In action is included all human behaviour when and insofar as the acting individual attaches subjective meaning. Action in this sense may be either overt or purely inward or subjective; it may consist of positive intervention in a situation, deliberately refraining from such intervention, or passively acquiescing. Action is social insofar as, by virtue of the subjective meaning attached to it by the acting individual, it takes account of the behaviour of others and is thereby oriented in its course. (Weber, 1978: 4)

Social action, for Weber, can be defined as occurring 'when the acting individual attaches a subjective meaning to an act and when it takes account of the behaviour of others and is thereby oriented in its course' (ibid.). The idea of 'interpretive understanding' and the concept of *Verstehen* is central to the theory of social action. In brief, *Verstehen* relates to 'human understanding'. In this sense, Weber believed that the job of social scientists was to examine the processes related to 'meaning' or 'understanding' in society. Weber concludes that a social phenomenon is identified not by its external characteristics but by its 'inner states', i.e. dependence on 'understanding' or *Verstehen.*

INTERPRETIVE SOCIOLOGY

The second concept in Weber's theory of social action is 'interpretive understanding'. For this, Weber distinguishes between two types of understanding: direct and explanatory or interpretive understanding (Weber, 1978: 8-12). According to Weber, the first type of understanding, i.e. direct understanding, refers to how individuals confirm actions in the world through observation. In this instance, the meaning of the act is evident from 'direct observation' of the physical characteristics of the act (ibid.). An example, Weber used to illustrate a direct understanding is the formula 2 × 2 = 4. This, he stated, involves direct understanding 'when we hear or read it' (ibid.).

The second type of understanding is explanatory or interpretive understanding. Explanatory understanding places the act within a context and assigns a motive. Weber tries to understand interpretative sociology with the help of interpretive understanding. Weber believed that individuals acted in and understood the social world only through interpretive acts. Although these acts involve assigning meanings to the given factual states in the outer world at the most fundamental level, Weber assumed that they must be products of the meaning states of actors.

Weber focuses on the mutual orientation of social actors and the 'understandable' motives of their actions, leading to his distinctiveness in his methodological approach. This type of understanding entails contextualizing the action to determine a motive.

SUBJECTIVE MEANING

To understand Weber's theory of social action, it is necessary to look at the various facets of subjective meaning. Weber argues that it takes place within the 'inner states' of the actor. Weber called this 'subjective meaning' to denote the actor's inner state, and it occurs out of range of the observation of others. Subjective meaning is interlinked with the interpretive understanding and *Verstehen*. In this sense, Weber stated:

> Something that is never attainable in the natural sciences is the subjective understanding of the action of the component individuals. On the other hand, the natural sciences cannot do this, being limited to formulating causal uniformity in objects and events and explaining individual facts by applying them. As distinguished from external observation, the additional explanation by interpretive understanding is attained only at a price—the more hypothetical and fragmentary character of results. Nevertheless, subjective understanding is the specific characteristic of sociological understanding. (Weber, 1978: 15)

Subjective meaning, therefore, is one of the essential elements of Weber's theory of social action. For him, action is social by virtue of the subjective meaning attached to it, and it takes place within the 'inner states' of the actor.

TYPES OF SOCIAL ACTION

Weber discusses four types of social action in his theory of social action. These are goal-oriented rational action *(Zweckrational)*, value-oriented (*Wertrational*), emotional or affective motivational, and traditional action.

The first type of social action is *traditional action*, according to Weber. In this type of action, the actor reacts 'automatically to habitual stimuli which guide behaviour in a course which has been repeatedly followed' (Weber, 1978: 25). Customs and traditions of the society regulate traditional actions. According to Weber, 'the great bulk of everyday action approaches this type, so far as customs fix both ends and means' (Morrison, 1995: 279-80). The lack of rational orientation exists in traditional action. Therefore, traditional action is classified as under the influence of long practices, customs, and habits. Priesthood abiding by church doctrine would be an example of this type of action.

The second type of action, according to Weber, is the *emotional* or *effectual* type of action. Action is effectual if it 'satisfies a need for revenge, sensual gratification, devotion, contemplative bliss, or the working off of emotional tensions' (Weber, 1978: 25). The means and ends of action are selected based on emotional criteria in this type of action. Since these actions are performed under certain emotions, these may or may not be rational. Like traditional action, effectual action is not oriented to a specific goal or value but expresses the actor's emotional state in a given circumstance. Participation in the religious services of a fundamentalist sect would be an example of this type of action.

Weber's third type of action is value-oriented rational action or *Wertrational.* The lack of rationality characterizes the first two types of social action, but the other two are mainly concerned with rational orientation. Value-oriented rational action is directed to overriding ideals of duty, honour or devotion to a cause. Here,the means of the action are chosen for their efficiency, but the ends are determined by value. In this type of action, actor seeks to 'put into practice their conviction of what seems to them to be required by duty, honour, the pursuit of beauty, a religious call, personal loyalty or the importance of some cause no matter in what it consists, regardless of the possible cost to themselves' (ibid.). The sole aim of value-oriented action is the realization of the value. Ascetic self-denial in the pursuit of holiness would be an example of this type of action.

The fourth type of action, according to Weber, is goal-oriented rational action or *Zweckrational.* This type differs from value-oriented rational action because 'the ends, the means, and the secondary results are rationally taken into account and weighed' (ibid.: 26). In this action, both goal and means are rationally chosen. In this action, the actor is free to choose the means of action purely in their rational efficacy. In addition to its rational orientation, *Zweckrational* is broader in scope and rationality than the other types of action. The most important characteristic of goal-oriented action is weighing means and ends, including the systematic taking into account 'alternative means to the ends, the relations of the end to the secondary consequences, and the relative importance of different possible ends' (ibid.). The action of an engineer is an example of this type who constructs a bridge by the most efficient technique.

Weber's classification of social action offers a comprehensive evaluation and understanding of rationality and the notion of means and ends. Meaningful actions are linked to *Wertrational* and *Zweckrational*. Both types of action are based on a rational understanding of means and ends, whereas, effectual and traditional are borderline cases. Therefore, it can be said that the notion of 'rationality' has a unique role to play in this context. At the same time, the classification of social action provides a unique direction to the types of authority, which is the basis of Weber's investigation of the course of western historical development.

III. WEBER'S SOCIOLOGY OF RELIGION

Weber's sociology of religion is considered an outstanding major work in sociology and the theory of religion. Weber's theory of religion appears in his famous writing *The Protestant Ethic and the Spirit of Capitalism* written between 1902 and 1903. Weber started writing *The Protestant Ethic and the Spirit of Capitalism* after completing a study of methodological issues in the social sciences. Two central themes are related to this work. First is the theme of religion and religious ideas; second is capitalism and capitalist development. Max Weber showed a deep interest in linking religious ideas and economic institutions in this work. Weber located a positive relationship between Protestant ethics and the spirit of Capitalism. The central aim of this work is the rationalization of religion. He traced the impact of Protestantism—primarily Calvinism—on the rise of the spirit of Capitalism.

To establish this theory of religion, Weber had two central aims in his mind. First, he wanted to show how beliefs influence action by establishing a connection between patterns of belief and the system of social action (Weber, 1958: 95). Second, Weber wanted to show a connection between religion and commercial activity. In this respect, capitalism was primarily shaped by religious forces, i.e. protestant ethics.

Weber's central thesis of the theory of religion is the concept of 'asceticism'.

> Historically, the term originates from religious piety expressed through self-denial and renunciation of worldly pleasure. As a religious doctrine, asceticism holds that self-discipline and self-denial can achieve a higher state. Hence, asceticism may be defined as a conscious denial of worldly pleasure to reach a valued goal and a higher moral state. (Morrison, 1995: 245)

Weber used this concept to explain two kinds of contradictory activities of Western capitalism: on the one hand, a devotion to amassing wealth beyond the personal needs of the individual and, on the other the avoidance of the use of wealth for personal pleasure or enjoyment. These two characteristics, i.e. the devotion to amassing wealth and an ascetic attitude toward pleasurable activity—led Weber to argue that if asceticism had found its way into commercial activity, then a religious ethic must underlie capitalism. Therefore, Weber used the concept of asceticism to pinpoint a way of living in the world in which the individual engages in self-denial to obtain future rewards (ibid.).

In fact, 'Weber, in his theory, did not directly link the idea system of the Protestant ethic to the structures of the capitalist system; instead, he was content to link the Protestant ethic to another system of ideas, the "spirit of capitalism"' (Ritzer, 1988: 133). In other words, Weber tried to look at the relationship of ideas rather than the system's basic structure. As a result, Weber rejected all the alternative explanations and theories of why capitalism arose in the West in the sixteenth and seventeenth centuries. Let us now discuss the ideas of the 'spirit of capitalism' and the 'Protestant ethic' and their relationship.

THE 'SPIRIT' OF CAPITALISM

The 'spirit' of capitalism is used by Weber to identify the unique characteristics of capitalist society that arise when religious doctrine becomes linked to economic practices.

Weber argued that three overriding demands could locate the spirit of capitalism: first, the devotion to amassing wealth and profit beyond the personal needs of the individual; second, the commitment to unrelieved toil and work coupled with self-denial; and third, the avoidance of the use of wealth for purposes of personal enjoyment. It is this 'spirit', according to Weber, that forms the unique nature of Western capitalism. Weber also discussed various types of capitalism: adventure capitalism, speculative capitalism, usurious capitalism, and modern capitalism (ascetic capitalism). Here 'spirit' of capitalism, according to Weber, is related to ascetic capitalism in the West (Weber, 1958: 27-8).

The spirit of capitalism involves several interrelated ideas. First, Weber's basic ideas of the spirit of capitalism have been drawn from Franklin's writing entitled *Necessary Hints to Those That Would Be Rich* and another work, *Advice to a Young Tradesman.* In this respect, Weber has drawn some of the essential points from Franklin's view:

> Remember that time is money. He that can earn ten shillings a day by his labour and goes abroad, or sits idle, one half of the day, though he spends but sixpence during his idleness, ought not to reckon that the only expense; he has really spent, or rather thrown away, five shillings besides.
>
> Remember that money is of the prolific, generating nature. Money can beget money, and its offspring can beget more, and so on. Five shillings turned is six, turned again is seven, three pence, and so on, till it becomes a hundred pounds. The more there is of it, the more it produces every turning so that the profits rise quicker and quicker. He that murders a crown destroys all that it might have produced, even scores of pounds.
>
> Remember this saying, The good paymaster is lord of another man's purse. He is known to pay punctually and exactly to the time he promises, may at any time, or any occasion, raise all the money his friends can spare. This is sometimes of great use. After industry and frugality, nothing contributes more to raising a young man in the world than punctuality and justice in his dealings; therefore, never keep borrowed money an hour beyond the time you promised.

> The trifling actions that affect a man's credit are to be regarded. The sound of your hammer at five in the morning, or eight at night, heard by a creditor, makes him easy six months longer; but if he sees you at a billiard table, or hears your voice at a tavern when you should be at work, he sends for his money the next day. It shows, besides, that you are mindful of what you owe; it makes you appear a careful and honest man, which still increases your credit. (1958: 49-50)

From the above discussion, the essential points of the spirit of capitalism may be summarized as follows:

1. Time is money,
2. Credit is money,
3. Money begets money,
4. One must be punctual in repaying the debt,
5. One should keep careful accounts of income and expenditure, and
6. One should always be known for prudence and industry.

In addition to Franklin's ideas, Weber thought that Protestantism, particularly Calvinism, was also crucial to the rise of the spirit of capitalism. In this regard, it is necessary to discuss the idea of Calvinism and the spirit of capitalism.

THE PROTESTANT ETHIC (CALVINISM) AND THE SPIRIT OF CAPITALISM

The Protestant ethic is a doctrine based on the notion of Calvinism. Weber argues that capitalism developed in countries where a particular variety of Protestantism, namely Calvinism, was robust. He argues that the sort of attitude to the world shaped by Calvinistic ideas provided individuals with the right kind of attitudes and motivations for bringing about a significant social change, the development of a capitalist society. The attitudes individuals required to bring about a capitalist society were the very attitudes inculcated by Calvinistic religion.

Calvinism, as an ethic, is founded by a French man John Calvin. In England, the followers of Calvin were known as the Puritans. Calvin's ideas had spread not only in England but also throughout Europe. Weber identified many significant ideas in Calvin's theological writings concerning capitalism's spirit.

Doctrine of Predestination

The doctrine of predestination is central to Calvinism. According to this view, God had divided all humanity into two classes of persons: the saved and the damned. He gave everlasting life, salvation, and eternal grace to those God had elected to be held. However, God withheld salvation and everlasting death and dishonour to those condemned (Troeltch, 1956: 100). Therefore, this idea is based on the fact that only a small number of people are chosen for salvation. In addition to this, 'Calvin introduced two stringent restrictions forbidding any reversal or exemption from the doctrine of predestination: (i) however God decided one's fate, there would be no hope of appeal and no possibility of change through traditional prayer, supplication or sacraments, (ii) God was transcendent and could not be called upon or approached, and thus was out of reach' (Morrison, 1995: 249). Therefore, Calvinists agreed that God was all-powerful and all-knowing. Thus, everyone's ultimate fate was predestined in the light of God's absolute knowledge.

Calvin's Image of God

God, according to Calvin, was powerful, and all-knowing. God's will was unknowable. God was transcendent and could not call upon an approach.

Calvinism and this-worldly Asceticism

Calvinism is related to the concept of asceticism. Here, asceticism refers to the view that self-discipline and self-denial can achieve a higher state. In Protestantism, Weber detected this-worldly asceticism. It recommends a simple lifestyle and hardwork for the people. Worldly or sensual pleasure, according to Calvinism, must be avoided for the glory of God. Protestant asceticism encouraged believers to practice self-denial. In this context, Protestantism had introduced regulation of everyday life, especially in worldly work.

In addition, Weber identified two historical types of asceticism: otherworldly asceticism and inner-worldly asceticism (1958: 541-4). Otherworldly asceticism renounces the world because it presents temptation. Here, salvation is sought after by a path to the otherworldly through religious devotion and self-denial (Morrison, 1995: 252). Otherworldly asceticism requires formal withdrawal from the world, 'from social and psychological ties with the family, from the possession of worldly goods, and political, economic, artistic, and erotic activities; in short, from all creaturely interests (Weber, 1958: 542). On the other hand, inner-worldly asceticism requires believers to focus their activities on the practice of self-denial in the world and to separate themselves from others in their minds. 'The inner-worldly ascetics thus see the world in terms of a test in which each individual becomes an "elect instrument of God" to perform good works on earth in a life of toil based on self-denial' (Morrison, 1995: 252).

The Notion of 'Calling'

The notion of 'calling' had a background in the catholic doctrine of the Middle Ages and referred to being called to a 'life task' of serving God as a vocation by performing ethical acts of devotion. 'The concept of "calling" indicates a transmission of ideas taking place between ethical and religious impulses in the outer-world of daily life and impulses in the inner-world of the conscience' (Morrison, 1995: 255). Therefore, the fulfilment of one's worldly duty became the only way for the Protestants so that their actions would be acceptable to God. In this sense, according to the Calvinist ethic, all work is equally important for the Protestants, and it should be performed with devotion and sincerity.

In brief, Weber summarized the Calvinist ethic in five points:

(a) There is a transcendent God who created the world and rules over it, which is incomprehensible and inaccessible to the finite minds of men.
(b) This all-powerful and mysterious God had predestined each of us to salvation or damnation so that we cannot by our works alter a divine decree which was made before we were born.
(c) God created the world for his glory.
(d) Whether he is to be saved or damned, man is obliged to work for the glory of God and to create the kingdom of God on earth.
(e) Earthly things, human nature, and flesh belong to the order of sin and death and salvation can come to man only through divine grace (Aron, 1967: 221-2).

In the last part of this theory, Weber summarized his position on Calvinism and its relation to capitalism as follows:

> The religious valuation of restless, continuous, systematic work in a worldly calling, as the highest means of asceticism, and at the same time, the surest and most evident proof of rebirth and genuine faith must have been the most powerful conceivable lever for the expansion of . . . the spirit of capitalism. (Weber, 1958: 172)

In addition to it, Weber also pointed out the interrelationship between Calvinism and the rise of capitalism. First, Calvinism provided the rising capitalist 'with sober, conscientious and unusually industrious workmen who clung to their work as to a life purpose willed by God' (1958: 177). Second, it legitimized an unequal stratification system by giving the capitalist the 'comforting assurances that the unequal distribution of this world's goods was a special dispensation of Divine Province' (ibid.).

Weber seeks further support for his hypothesis by exploring the relationship between religious ideas and economic ideas and behaviour in the West, India, China, and Israel. In this sense, Weber made a point for other societies that capitalism did not arise because of Calvinist ethics and the spiritual and material barriers.

IV. CLASS, STATUS AND PARTY

Weber's theory of social class, status group, and power is central to his writing and related to economic, social, and political aspects. It was written between 1911 and 1920 and appeared in the second volume of *Economy and Society*. In this context, Abraham stated: 'In the formation of relationships, says Weber, men tend to be attracted to and enter into social relationships with others who share common positions and interests in the area of economics, politics and culture' (Abraham & Morgan, 1985: 183). Thus, class, status, and power are considered three dimensions of Weber's social stratification.

First, Weber put forward his theory of social class based on three distinct categories: (i) class with market situation; (ii) class concerning different types of social action flowing from class interests; and (iii) the formation of social classes concerning historical types of class struggle (Morrison, 1995: 233).

Weber defined the concept of class concerning the market. He stated that 'a class is several people having a specific causal component of life chances in common. This component is represented by economic interests in possession of goods and opportunities for income under the market conditions' (Weber, 1968: 927). From this definition, two things appeared: *life chances* and *market*. By class, Weber refers to the economic order of society where 'market relationships' were of the utmost importance. This concept of Weber's class is very close to the 'objective' part of Marx's concept of class. Weber's definition of class also refers to a 'class situation determined by life chances which may arise when individuals sell skills and services on the market' (Morrison, 1995: 233). On the other hand, the class situation is also determined by the ownership of usable property, which creates returns on investments and incomes in the form of rent (Weber, 1968: 928). These two class situations, viz., property and the opportunities arising from incomes define the class situation of modern society.

CONCEPT OF STATUS

The second dimension of power, according to Weber, is the development of the 'status group' in modern society. The concept of the status group has a significant role in his theory of class and stratification. By 'status', Weber talks about how the organization of society produces different amounts of prestige or social honour for other groups of individuals. The status situation is a fundamental concept to understand status in social activity. Weber defined a status situation as 'every component of life fate determined by a positive or negative social estimation of honour' (Weber, 1968: 932). Therefore, the status situation is determined by a specific—positive or negative—social honour. Members of status groups are held together by notions of proper lifestyles or consumption patterns and social esteem or honour.

In addition, Weber also made a distinction between class-situation and status-situation. Weber explained the class situation for the market. In contrast to a class situation, the status situation is defined by its 'strict separation' from the economic order and the market sphere and, in this sense, is functionally separate from class (Weber, 1968: 937). Class is restricted to the market sphere and characterized by acquisition, whereas status is outside and characterized by consumption. Both class and status are considered separate dimensions of the stratification system. In this sense, a particular social group's highest prestige (status) does not always belong to the richest (class).

Weber outlined four distinct characteristics of status groups and their function within society. First status groups, he stated: (i) evaluate the social worth and bestow honour; (ii) segregate themselves from another status group; (iii) uphold patterns of consumption and canons of taste; and (iv) monopolise status privileges (Morrison, 1995: 240). Weber designated a status situation for the first characteristic of a status group as determined by a 'positive or negative evaluation of honour' (1968: 936). The second characteristic of social groups is segregation. Weber thought that the status group sets itself apart from other groups regarding lifestyle and social badges (ibid.: 933-4). The Indian caste system is an example of this category. A third characteristic of the status group is the privileges associated with it. Weber stated that status groups create 'monopolisation of material and ideal goods' (ibid.: 935). The British royal family is an example of this category.

Another fact related to it is that status groups form communities with shared interests and purposes. 'These are based on shared conditions and a common perspective derived from the similar experience of lifestyle and taste habits' (Morrison, 1995: 242-3). Therefore, it can be said that status groups are usually considered communities.

CONCEPT OF PARTY

Parties are the third dimension of power and stratification system. Parties may be formed based on classes or status groups or a mixture of both. The concept of parties is found only in complex societies. In fact, 'political parties are restricted to the realm of power and the political order' (Morrison, 1995: 243). The action of parties is oriented toward two kinds of activities: first, the acquisition of power, and second, the influencing of the actions of others for political purposes (Weber, 1968: 938). The key purpose, according to Weber, of political parties is to secure power and maintain separation from the economic and social spheres. In brief, parties are the groupings of people oriented toward acquiring social power.

Weber tried to understand the complexes of social stratification from class to bureaucratic organization in modern society. Third, Weber thought it was a type of movement from class to authority to bureaucracy to understand the nature and function of power in modern society. Finally, Weber proposed legitimate authority through the bureaucratic coordination of activities based on rational principles to regulate modern society.

V. POWER, AUTHORITY AND LEGITIMACY

Weber's theory of power, authority (domination), and legitimacy are essential parts in the first volume of *Economics and Society* which came out in 1914. The main aim of Weber's work was to see how political power manifested itself in different historical contexts. Generally, he used the terms 'domination' and 'authority' interchangeably in his discussion. Both derive from the German word *Herrschaft*. Raymond Aron defines, *Herrschaft* as the master's ability to obtain the obedience of those who theoretically owe it to him. Weber's concept of *Herrschaft* is used for 'authority' or 'domination'.

Weber began his theoretical discussion by distinguishing between power and domination. Power is the ability of individuals to carry out their will in a situation, despite resistance. Domination, by contrast, refers to the right of a ruler within an 'established order' to issue commands to others and expect them to obey (Morrison, 1995: 283). Therefore, power involves the ability to influence and control the behaviour of others even against their will. Weber defines power as the likelihood that an individual will realize his or her will in a situation of social action. In this regard, power is transformed into authority or domination when it gets legitimacy or willing obedience to the governors. Weber argues that people obey authority when they view it as legitimate. Weber aimed to focus on various systems of domination rather than power. In light of this, legitimacy became important in the analysis of authority. Each system of authority is based on some corresponding belief of people in legitimacy.

The concept of legitimacy is mainly dealt with by Weber in his theory of legitimate domination to indicate 'the extent to which officials, groups and individuals actively acknowledge the validity of a ruler in the established order and the right of a ruler to issue commands'. In modern society, the law is a basis of political legitimacy. Legitimacy may be claimed based on charismatic, traditional, and rational grounds. On these grounds, Weber identifies three types of authority (domination): (1) Charismatic domination, (2) Traditional domination, and (3) Rational-legal domination.

CHARISMATIC DOMINATION (AUTHORITY)

The first type of domination, according to Weber, is charismatic domination. The concept of charisma characterizes charismatic domination. Charisma is a gift of divine grace. Weber used Charismatic authority to refer to a people having extraordinary influencing power over many people. Charismatic leaders are believed to have capabilities that are not accessible to ordinary individuals, and their powers are regarded as having a divine origin. On this basis, the individual is treated as a leader. Such individuals can be saints, prophets, heroes in war, famous political leaders, and social reformers. Charismatic leaders are Kabir, Nanak, Jesus, Mohammed, Mahatma Gandhi, Rajaram Mohan Roy, and Vivekananda. Some of the crucial elements or concepts are involved in charismatic domination. These are:

Recognition of Duty

This 'recognition of duty' is key to the followers' belief that they should practice the charismatic leader's vision. In this way, the type of action that the charismatic authority is related to is affective action. The followers are in a highly charged emotional state due to the teachings and appeal of the charismatic leaders.

Renunciation of the Past

It is a characteristic of charisma that can mobilize legitimacy. In this respect, it may be associated with a revolutionary force for change. He suggests that charismatic domination tends to reject the desires and needs of everyday life. Thus, we can say that these leaders rejected all the conventional social obligations and norms. 'This serves to create the appearance that the leader is "above" everyday needs and routines and adopts an ascetic way of life.'

Routinization of Charisma

Weber used routinization to refer to when a charismatic leader gets transformed from charismatic leadership into institutionalized leadership. Here office becomes the focus of authority rather than an individual. In this context, the original charisma gets transformed into traditional or rational-legal authority. This situation arises with the death or disappearance of a charismatic leader. As a result, a new person takes that leader's position who may not have charismatic power. To transmit the original message of that leader, some organization develops, and finally, it takes the shape of the routinization of charisma. In short, charismatic authority, therefore, is based on the normative patterns prescribed by the individual possessing charisma.

TRADITIONAL AUTHORITY (DOMINATION)

Traditional authority is, according to Weber, the second type of domination. Traditional authority depends on traditional legitimacy. It follows from traditional action. Traditional authority is regulated by tradition and custom, on the 'sanctity of age-old rules and powers'. In traditional authority, rulers or leaders enjoy personal authority under their inherited status. It is seen as legitimate in the light of customary rights and traditional norms. Monarchies and lords of feudal estates are historical examples of traditional systems of domination.

In traditional domination, two formal types of traditional systems are found. First is the patrimonial system, which is common in feudal societies. In the patrimonial system of domination, the landlord may rule entirely without administrative staff. This system tends to be based on a 'system of favourites' who perform functions for rulers out of loyalty or obligation. The master regulates this system in the decision-making process of any type of dispute. The second type of system identified by Weber in traditional domination is patriarchalism. The central characteristic of patriarchalism is the belief that authority is exercised by 'joint right' and in the interest of all members (Morrison, 1995). This form of system is found in households where the master obtains legitimacy and governs by the rule of inheritance.

In brief, traditional authority is characterized by customs and traditions rather than legal rules. 'Traditional authority issues command based on what Weber called the "edict". Edicts may be defined as a personal decree issued by a leader reflecting the "arbitrary" nature of traditional powers' (Morrison, 1995: 372).

RATIONAL-LEGAL AUTHORITY

The third type of authority discussed by Weber is rational-legal authority. Rational-legal authority is based on rational legitimacy. In this, authority issue commands based on principles of law rather than the leader's authority or any custom and tradition. Established legal rules and regulations guide it. 'Since the operation and organization of this system of domination take the form of legality, the total system of laws and judicial framework leads to a form of administrative organization which grows out of the principle of legality' (Morrison, 1995: 372). It is practiced by administrative staff who operate under specific written rules and laws. Those who exercise authority are appointed based on their required qualifications.

Weber maintained that legal domination exists and creates legitimacy under the statute. Therefore, rational-legal authority is regulated by well-defined law (established by the legislative body) based on rational understanding. Bureaucracy is a good example of rational-legal authority in modern times. Thus, bureaucracy is the medium through which rational-legal authority is practiced.

VI. WEBER'S STUDY OF BUREAUCRACY

Weber's work on bureaucracy first appeared in his study on the *Economics of Antiquity* in 1908, and he discussed the central part of bureaucracy in *Economy and Society*. He studied bureaucracy as a part of the theory of domination which appeared in part one of *Economy and Society*. Weber tried to trace out the development of the modern means of administration. In this context, 'Weber identified six types of bureaucratic structure: (i) states which tend to control policy and policing functions; (ii) ecclesiastical communities which are required to administer to large populations of believers; (iii) economies whose main function is to distribute goods and coordinate functions; (iv) the modern agency; (v) the military; and (vi) the judiciary.'

Weber's main aim in this study is to see the various perspectives and aspects of historical understanding of bureaucratization in the development of modern society. In this context, he made comparisons of administratively oriented societies such as the administration of early Egypt and Rome, Asiatic societies, and Central Europe. Based on this comparison, Weber made it clear that 'Egypt was not a bureaucratically organized society'. In contrast, European feudal societies were characterized by the 'patrimonial system of administration' with several administrative characteristics. In the patrimonial system, power was controlled and regulated by customary rights rather than written law. Based on comparing different administrative run societies, he outlined some points. First, the seat of administrative activity shifts from the households to the office set up arrangements. Second, administrative procedures shifted from customary rules to strictly legal rules. Third, administrative authority shifted from lords or masters to jurisdictional authority based on hierarchically oriented positions. Fourth, administrators were not bound by written rules or laws in previous societies but by prescribed rules and regulations in modern societies.

FACTORS LEADING TO BUREAUCRATIZATION

Weber reasoned that several changes in different historical periods led to the development of bureaucratic organizations based on rational-legal authority. First, changes occur in the conditions and organization of society. At this point, industrialization played a significant role in machines-oriented work, rational planning of activities, etc. Second, changes occur in the system of rationality and decision making. Industrial and commercial enterprises' rational understanding and decision making processes rationalize everyday life and industrial production. The third was developing a system of 'calculable law' and legislation. This led to the accountability and rationalization of commercial work and administration.

CONCEPT AND CHARACTERISTICS OF BUREAUCRACY

Weber used bureaucracy to denote the development of a modern means of administration. It was an outcome of historical and social processes. Weber's bureaucracy is based on rational-legal authority. According to Weber, bureaucracy is a social organization based on hierarchical order. It aims to rationalize the administration of states or other organizations such as working for science and technology and industrial and commercial ventures in modern societies. Weber believes that bureaucracy has a very close relationship with democracy. For this, he constructs ideal types of bureaucracy and accepts the universality of bureaucracy in modern society. According to him,'only bureaucracy has provided the foundation for the means of administration based on rational law "systematized based on statutes" eliminating irrational considerations in the application of expediency'. After giving a brief overview of bureaucracy, Weber attributed the following characteristics to bureaucracy:

1. A bureaucratic administration is based on a hierarchy of officials in authority. This organization follows a clearly defined structure of offices and positions, with duly assigned responsibilities. In a bureaucracy, decision-making is based on the levels of authority and jurisdiction. Thus, for example, lower officials are supervised by higher ones and are answerable to them.
2. Specified rules and legislation regulate the system of bureaucracy. Therefore, everybody has to work based on his/her status in the office. In other words, the regular activities associated with each status are distributed fixedly as official duties.
3. The rights and duties of officials are explicitly prescribed and proscribed in written regulations that have been adequately 'enacted'. This results in staff members owing their allegiance to the system of impersonal legal rules rather than to the caprice of superiors.
4. Every official receives a contractually fixed salary based on his/her position or status in the administrative system. This creates a clear distinction between the bureaucratic organization and the individual's private affairs.
5. The bureaucratic system applies impersonal guidelines for dealing with work responsibilities. Therefore, official work is no longer a secondary activity but something that demands the total working capacity of the official.
6. Bureaucratic organization is based on a division of labour on specialized functions and responsibilities. Authority is strictly defined, and officials obey orders only from those immediately above them in rank.

7. The management of the bureaucratic office is carried out through written documents or files. They are preserved and kept by clerks specially appointed for this purpose.
8. Selection in a bureaucratic system for employment and promotion is based on their technical knowledge, skill, and performance. Therefore, the officials are protected against the whims and caprices of their bosses and political masters. Consequently, they can act rationally and according to rules.
9. In a bureaucratic system, the appointment of employees is by a higher official, rather than any political approach or election.
10. In a bureaucratic administration, the discharge of responsibilities is based on calculable rules, which are carried out 'without regard for persons'.

In addition, the concept of the office is one of the essential characteristics of Weber's study of bureaucracy. By 'office', Weber meant a sphere of legal authority granted to an area of work under the administrative jurisdiction of an official and his or her directives. Thus, bureaucracy in office may be characterized as follows:

(i) Office work is a 'vocation' for officials.
(ii) Office-holders are required to undergo 'prescribed courses of training which require their total attention for a long period'.
(iii) Officials perform their responsibilities as 'duties' executed as administrative functions. In this sense, they are expected to do their work honestly.
(iv) Officials qualifications, technical knowledge and skills determine their position or rank in the office.
(v) Officials are outside the ownership over the means of production.
(vi) Loyalty to the office-based on legal rules is necessary to maintain.

Therefore, the official bureaucratic functions within a sphere of legal authority, a degree of social responsibility, are associated with offices holding. Weber further discusses bureaucratization and rationalization of modern western economies in the following words:

> Under otherwise similar conditions, a 'societal action', methodically ordered and led, is superior to every resistance to 'mass' or 'communal action'. Furthermore, where the bureaucratization of administration has been thoroughly carried through, a form of power relation is established that is practically unshatterable.

In the final section of Weber's theory of Bureaucracy, he examined the social consequences of bureaucratization. He outlined two broad categories of consequence. The first is the incompatibility of democracy with bureaucratic development. In a bureaucracy, the governed tend to accept bureaucratic decision making without question and thus give up the right to accountable governance. The second consequence of bureaucracy is the tendency to develop secrecy. The bureaucratic organization is based on specific rules. Therefore, the bureaucrats must maintain the confidentiality of their knowledge and their intentions.

In brief, bureaucracy is considered more efficient in performing its assigned tasks based on rational-legal authority. Bureaucracy as a form of administration is characterized by continuity, hierarchy, specified rules and regulations, record-based, salaried employment. Bureaucracy is understood as a very effective regulative instrument of modern society.

VII. RATIONALITY AND RATIONALIZATION

Weber's concept of rationality and the process of rationalization are central to his theoretical and conceptual understanding. He used protestantism, capitalism, bureaucracy, social action, and ideal type construction concepts. He also discusses the notion of rationality in sociological investigation and value-free sociology. Rationality refers to those ideas and behaviour which are logical and consistent and applicable to empirical knowledge. A rationalization is a process in which rationality is analysed in several aspects and activities of life.

The conviction that rationality is the distinctive characteristic of human beings has been a central theme in Western philosophy for over two hundred years (Mitchell, 1968: 142).

According to Weber, modern society is characterized by rationality. Rationality and the process of rationalization are related to rational action. Weber thought in the modern world, all spheres of society, the economic, political, and legal spheres, underwent rationalization. To Weber, rationalization means that 'principally there are no mysterious incalculable forces that come into play, but rather one can, in principle, master all things by calculation. One need no longer have recourse to magical means to master or implore the spirits, as did the savage, for whom such mysterious power existed' (Hearn, 1985: 76). Rationalization depends on two types of activities: (i) social action strategies; and (ii) adjustments of the means and ends of action in attaining goals.

Weber distinguishes between the concept of rationality and the process of rationalization. Weber referred to various ways to understand rationality in terms of 'economic rationality', 'instrumental rationality', 'value rationality', and 'formal and substantive rationality' (Kalberg, 1980: 1145-79). On the other hand, Weber discusses different forms of rationality and categorizes them into four broad types: formal, substantive, practical, and theoretical. Hence, 'rationalization refers to the overall historical process by which reality is increasingly mastered by calculation, scientific knowledge, and rational action'. Weber accepts that action in modern society is based on the actor's orientation and the social situation of action. Thus, scientists, lawyers, administrators, and policymakers may have different forms of rationality.

Weber (Kalberg, 1980: 1145-79) discussed four types of rationality in his work: (i) formal, (ii) substantive, (iii) practical, and (iv) theoretical or technical.

(i) *Formal Rationality:* The first and most important type of rationality is formal rationality. It involves means-ends calculation. Weber used this term to design the amount of quantitative calculation and accounting procedures into action or decision. Formal rationality occurs concerning 'universally pragmatic self-interests, and regulation'. Bureaucracy and rational-legal authority-based systems may be considered formal rationality. This form of rationality is also found in economic, legal, political, and scientific situations. It is because of universally applied rules, laws, and regulations. Weber described capitalism and bureaucracies as 'two great rationalizing forces'.

(ii) *Substantive Rationality:* The second form of rationality directly orders action into patterns through clusters of values. Weber used this term to refer to the degree to which action is shaped by an orientation to values regardless of the nature of the ends or outcome of an action. 'Substantive rationality involves a choice of means to ends within the context of a compatible system of values.' In other words, any compatible value system is substantively rational. Weber believed that formal and substantive rationality is opposed and that, ultimately substantive rationality views formal rationality as inimical to its purpose.

(iii) *Practical Rationality:* The third form of rationality discussed by Weber is practical rationality. Kalberg defined practical rationality as 'every way of life that views and judges worldly activity about the individual's purely pragmatic and egoistic interests'. People who practice practical rationality accept given reality. Within the framework of practical rationality, all the means of procuring desired ends are viewed as 'techniques' or strategies rather than as systems of values that are adhered to based on ethical standards or criteria of action. It means practical rationality is concerned with 'techniques' based means to get desired ends. Practical rationality does not believe in religious ideas and metaphysical, philosophical interpretations of either means or ends.

(iv) *Theoretical Rationality:* The last or fourth type of rationality is theoretical rationality. 'Theoretical rationality

> involves a cognitive effort to master reality through increasingly abstract concepts rather than through action.' Theoretical rationality imposes on reality in terms of induction, deduction, etc. Theoretical rationality acts by producing an 'image of the world' employing abstract concepts and conceptualization. The shift from practical to theoretical rationality leads to a departure from the concrete world to the world of abstraction. The aim is that the actor transcends daily realities to understand the world as a meaningful cosmos. The effect of theoretical rationality on action is limited. Theoretical rationality undertakes an orientation to reality in the realm of theoretical understanding.

In addition to differentiating among four types of rationality, Kalberg explains Weber about organized ways of life. 'Practical rationality lacks this ability because it involves reactions to situations rather than efforts to order them. Theoretically, theoretical rationality is cognitive and has a highly limited ability to suppress practical rationality and seems to be more of an end-product than a producer' (Kalberg, 1980: 1145-79). Hence, the subjugation of practical rationality leads to the development of formal rationality due to the enormous emphasis on methodical ways of life.

VIII. CONCLUSION

Max Weber is considered one of the founding fathers of sociology. Compared with Marx and Durkheim, Weber's approach was more individualist. Analysis of the different structures of modern society is the central thrust of the study. His contributions to sociology are methodological approach, capitalism, sociology of religion, social stratification, and rationality. However, Weber himself was opposed to creating a professorship in sociology. Instead, he tries to find the solution to any problem from a contextual viewpoint.

Weber's methodological approach to sociology was directly related to the *Methodenstreit* of the German debate about the proper method for the social sciences. *Verstehen*, interpretive understanding, subjective meaning, and ideal-type construction are central to Weber's methodological orientation. Weber mainly focuses on how social reality can be understood and explained from the entire analysis. In this sense, he tries to see a social situation or problem or phenomenon based on contextual reality. And hence causal functional relation can be traced out based on concentrating on a particular case. At the same time, he evaluates any phenomena from the actor's point of view. Weber applied his methodological approach in analysing social action, religion, and capitalism, bureaucracy, class, status, party, etc. Here, he tried to study meaningful human actions concerning society properly.

In the analysis of social change, he did not accept that a single factor is responsible for it. However, Max Weber was undoubtedly influenced by Marx in his thought of economic interpretation of society. As Parsons puts it,

> Undoubtedly, the main starting point of Weber's descriptive treatment was Marx. Marx's writings and the discussions of capitalism and socialism revolving around them made a profound impression in Germany in Weber's formative period. Still, typically enough, it was the 'Historical' Marx and not the Marx, who was most closely related to the classical economic theory.

Although Max Weber tried to present sociology with a scientific look, he has also been subjected to a good deal of criticism. He has been charged with being weak towards Functionalism. Weber has been criticized for emphasizing an individualistic and subjective understanding of a social phenomenon in this context. His analysis of the relationship between religion and capitalism has also been attacked. In this respect, Sorokin has quoted an example of Japan where no progress worth the name was made in the field of religion. Still, it had miraculous improvement in the economic, political, and cultural areas. On this, Sorokin has criticized Max Weber as follows: 'Nevertheless Weber very often slips from his functional standpoint into that of one causation.' However, despite his weak points in the analysis of society, it cannot be denied that he made a precious contribution to sociological thought, theories, methodology, and so on. These contributions of Weber would carry sociology in a forward direction to a greater extent.

KEY TERMS

Action: Behaviour has meaning to the individual, that is, behaviour that he/she directs toward a goal.

Social Action Theory: A theoretical development within social behaviour focused on social action. The primary influence in the development of social action theory was the work of Max Weber. In social action theory, human behaviour is studied in terms of persons acting in culturally defined situations and systems of social relationships.

Social Action: Action-oriented to or influenced by another person or persons. Max Weber pointed out that the failure to act, or the passive acquiescence to the actions of others, is included as a part of social action.

Asceticism: A way of life-based on devotion to specific non-material values or ideals with a renunciation of physical pleasures and an emphasis on simplicity, discipline, and self-denial.

Authority: Legitimate power is considered an authority when institutionalized in a society or social system. This form of power is attached to social status and is accepted as proper and legitimate by all social system members. Systems of authority are particularly characteristic of formal organizations, but positions of authority are also found in small groups. Weber categorized authority into three types: traditional authority, charismatic authority and rational-legal authority.

Charismatic Authority: The term given by Max Weber is based on the notion of 'charisma', i.e. the grace of God. Hence, charismatic authority is legitimatized by a leader's extraordinary characteristics and mission's inspired or sanctified nature.

Rational-legal: Weber used this term in his political theory to describe a form of legitimate domination resting on the belief that rules are enacted by due process and founded upon basic legal precepts. Rational legal authority arises in societies with a developed industry system, markets, and bureaucratic administration.

Traditional Authority: A term used by Weber to denote a system of domination whose claim to legitimacy is based on the 'sanctity of old rules' and customs.

Bureaucracy: A large scale, formal organization that is highly differentiated and efficiently organized employing formal rules and departments or bureaus of highly trained experts whose activities are coordinated by a hierarchical chain of command. This type of organization is also characterized by the centralization of authority and emphasis on discipline, rationality, technical knowledge, and impersonal procedures. Beyond the formal characteristics of bureaucracy, Weber put forward a theory of bureaucratic development in which he linked the rise of bureaucracy with the emergence of legal domination.

Bureaucratization: The process in which a formal organisation increasingly takes on the characteristics of a bureaucracy. A central aspect of this process is the formalization of rules and regulations. Bureaucratization may proceed to any degree for a given organization.

Calling: Following a profession or doing work as a sacred duty that God called an individual to do.

Calvinism: A branch of Protestantism that began with the theological teaching of John Calvin.

Charisma: A mystical quality of a personality that makes an individual seem to possess specific extraordinary abilities and advantages. Weber borrowed this term, literally meaning 'gift of grace', from the Christian concept of extraordinary power inherent in the priesthood.

Class: Weber used social class to refer to groups who 'share the same causal component of life chances'.

Formal Rationality: A term used by Weber to indicate the amount of calculation and accounting procedure that goes into an action to increase its efficacy. Formal rationality imposes order on the world through a system of measurement and calculable activity.

Ideal Type: A conceptualization or mental construct composed of characteristic elements of a class of phenomena used in social analysis. The ideal type was developed as an essential methodological technique by Max Weber in conjunction with his method of *Verstehen*. A heuristic device is used to describe, compare, and test hypotheses relating to empirical reality.

Induction: The logical process in which generalizations are inferred from specific facts. Induction is the process of reasoning from individual instances to general principles. The experimental method is inductive.

Interpretive Sociology: This term is used to define a body of social theory devised by Weber to make valid judgements about actors' 'inner states' in their actions with others in a constituted social environment. Weber believed that individuals only act in and understand the social world through interpretive acts. Thus, he thought that the processes of assigning meaning to the factual states of the outer world are evidence of the 'inner states' of actors who rely on their understanding (*Verstehen*) of the acts of others.

Legitimacy: This is a term used by Weber in his theory of legitimate authority to indicate the extent to which officials, groups and individuals actively acknowledge the validity of a ruler in an established order and the right of a ruler to issue commands.

Means and End of Action: This term is used throughout Weber's writings to indicate the various degree of rationality of social action and the extent to which these rationalities serve as guides to realizing goals. Weber believed that human action could be understood as 'means-ends' rationality. In this case, the 'means' refer to the methods or procedures individuals use to attain goals and achieve tasks, whereas 'ends' refer to the aims or purposes of action. Modern society effects change in the means-ends scheme.

Party: This term is used in Weber's political sociology to refer to the sphere of activities appropriate to political parties. Political parties are oriented toward the acquisition of power and the influencing of the actions of others for political purposes.

Power: A term used by Weber to describe the state of affairs in which individuals can carry out their own will over others 'despite resistance'. Weber defines power as the likelihood that an individual will realize his or her will in a situation of social action.

Predestination: This term is used by Weber to denote a religious doctrine propagated by John Calvin in the sixteenth century. The idea of predestination is central to protestant ethics.

Protestant Ethic: The concept was discussed by Max Weber, who tried to show the ideological compatibility of rational capitalism and Protestantism. This ethic was very supportive of the development of modern rational capitalism. The primary roots of this idea were first developed by Martin Luther and then by John Calvin.

Puritanism: Weber used this term in his study of capitalism to identify an attitude that protestants develop toward life primarily based on the notion of self-denial and antagonism toward sensuous experience. In addition, Puritanism presupposes individual autonomy in spiritual matters and the commitment to purge the church of catholic influences.

Rational: Weber used the term rational to refer to: (i) types of social order, and (ii) orientations to social actions. In the first case, rational societies demonstrate calculable law, rational commerce, and a practical orientation to reality. Rational refers to various means-ends calculations that increase practical outcomes and social goals concerning an orientation to social action.

Rationalization: Weber used rationalization to describe how an orientation increasingly masters nature, society, and individual action to planning, technical procedure and rational action. Thus, rationalization depends on social action strategies and adjustments to the means and ends of action in attaining goals.

Rationality: Refers to a standard of action whose substance lies in weighing means and ends. Weber essentially used the term to describe an orientation to reality that systematically weighs up means and ends purposes of efficacy and the practical attainment of goals. Weber believed that different types of rationality become dominant at various stages social development, eliminating other orientations to reality such as magic, prayer or oracular considerations. Thus, rationality, with particular reference to social action, can be of two types: (i) *Subjective Rationality*, referring to the degree of inner evaluation which the actor engages in cognitively before an act; and (ii) *objective rationality*, which refers to the degree to which action embodies rational principles by adhering to formal norms or specific means-ends calculations.

Routinization: It is a transformation process of charismatic authority into traditional or rational-legal authority.

Social Spheres: Weber used the term social sphere to indicate different realms in a society whose existence, activities, ideas, and rationality: (i) create orientations for social action; and (ii) impart influences and modes of development to other social realms.

Sola Fide: This is a term used by Weber to describe the particular features of protestant religious doctrine that advocate private solitude in religious faith.

Spirit of Capitalism: A term used to identify the unique characteristics of capitalist society which arise when religious doctrine become linked to economic practices. The spirit of capitalism developed only in modern western capitalism.

State: Weber defined the state as a rational institution characterized by law, a rational economy and a bureaucratic administration.

Status Group: A status group may be defined as one whose members share the same 'life fate' component as determined by a positive or negative estimation of honour or social worth.

Subjective: Weber used the term to identify an order of events related to human social action. The term 'subjective' refers to human 'inner states' and is intended to restrict itself from the purely outward behaviour of individuals.

Substantive Rationality: It refers to the degree to which an orientation shapes action to 'ultimate values'. According to Weber, substantive rationality is not restricted to the straightforward attainment of goals but applies values shaped by ethical, utilitarian or egalitarian standards. Thus, substantive rationality always upholds 'value scales' and adheres to social justice, ethics, and equality principles.

Technical Rationality: Weber used the term to indicate an orientation to reality, stressing a systematic evaluation and consideration of the means and end of action for specific outcomes. The highest form of technical rationality is the scientific experiment, which calculates stress to achieve particular ends or results.

This-worldly Asceticism: Asceticism applied to worldly affairs or rigorous self-discipline in day-to-day life. This was the characteristic attitude of the early protestants, according to Weber. He contrasted it with other worldly asceticism in religions like Hinduism. Here, individuals discipline themselves to renounce the world through penance, austerities, etc.

Value Neutrality: Weber used this term in his methodological studies to (i) indicate the necessary objectivity required by a researcher in solving problems in the social sciences; and (ii) the caution investigators should exercise against making 'value judgements' that coincide with the particular orientation or motives of the researcher.

Value Orientation: A value to which an individual is committed and influences his behaviour. Value orientation may be said that the group members share a specific value, but this value will not be equally important.

Value Relevance: Weber used this term to refer to the means by which specific aspects of reality are brought to the attention of scientific observers and isolated as a matter of investigative interest. Thus, the principle of value relevance is a way of dealing with the claim that the natural sciences select what is of research interest solely based on its objective scientific merit.

Verstehen: Verstehen means 'understanding'. This term is used by Weber in a theory of social action. Weber employed the term to convey what he thought was unique about the subject matter of the social sciences. The social sciences are concerned with actors 'inner-states' who act on their 'understanding' (*Verstehen*).

REFERENCES

Abraham, Francis and John Henry Morgan, *Sociological Thought from Comte to Sorokin*, Macmillan, Madras, 1985.

Anchor, Robert, 'Heinrich Rickert', *The Encyclopedia of Philosophy*, Collier-Macmillan, London, 2013.

Aron, Raymond, *Main Currents in Sociological Thought*, vol. 2, Basic Books, New York, 1967.

——, *Main Currents in Sociological Thought*, vol. II, Doubleday, Garden City, 1970.

Beck, Lewis White, 'Neo-Kantianism', *The Encyclopedia of Philosophy*, vol. 5, Macmillan, New York, 1967.

Bleicher, Josef, *Contemporary Hermeneutics: Hermeneutics as Method, Philosophy and Critique*, Routledge and Kegan Paul, London, 1980.

Brunn, H.H., *Science, Values and Politics in Max Weber's Methodology*, Munksgaard, Copenhagen, 1972.

Coser, Lewis A., *Masters of Sociological Thought*, Rawat Publications, Jaipur, 1996.

Frank, R.I., Translator's introduction to Max Weber, *The Agrarian Sociology of Ancient Civilizations*, NLB, London, 1976.

Hearn, F., *Reason and Freedom in Sociological Thought*, Allen and Unwin: Boston, 1985.

Kalberg, Stephen, *Max Weber's Types of Rationality: Cornerstones for the Analysis of Rationalization Processes in History*. Chicago Journal, vol. 85, no. 5, March 1980, pp. 1145-79.

Marx and Weber: *Alienation and Rationalization*. The . . . https://socandcrim.wordpress.com/2017/03/06/marx-and-weber-alienation-and-rationalization/

Mitchell, G.D. (ed.), *A Dictionary of Sociology*, Routledge and Kegan Paul, London, 1968.

Morrison, *Marx, Durkheim, Weber: Formation of Modern Social Thought*, Sage Publications, London, 1995.

Mueller-Vollmer, Kurt, 'Language, Mind and Artifact: An Outline of Hermeneutic Theory since the Enlightenment', in K. Mueller-Vollmer (ed.), *The Hermeneutics Reader*, Continuum, New York, 1985, pp. 1-53.

Rickert, Heinrich, *Science, and History: A Critique of Positivist Epistemology* (trans. George Reisman), D. Van Nostrand, Princeton, 1962.

Ritzer, *Sociological Theory*, McGraw Hill Pub. Com., Singapore, 1988.

Rossides, Daniel W., *The History and Nature of Sociological Theory*, Houghton Mifflin Company, Boston, 1978.

Shills, Edward and Henry Finch (eds.), *Max Weber on the Methodology of the Social Sciences*, The Free Press, New York, 1949.

Tribe, Keith (ed.) *Reading Weber*, Routledge, London, 1989.

Troeltch, Ernst, *The Social Teaching of the Christian Churches*, Allen and Unwin, London, 1956.

Weber, Marianne, *Max Weber: A Biography*, John Wiley & Sons, New York, 1975.

Weber, Max, 'Ideal Types', in K. Thompson and J. Junstall (eds.), *Sociological Perspectives*, Penguin Books, Middle-sex, p. 63 (63-7), 1972.

——, 'Objectivity in Social Science and Social Policy', in E.A. Shils and H. Finch (eds.), *Max Weber on the Methodology of the Social Sciences*, The Free Press, New York, 1949, pp. 50-112.

——, *Economy and Society*, 3 vols., Bedminster Press, Totowa, N.J., (1921) 1968.

——, G. Roth and C. Wittich (eds.), *Economy and Society*, University of California Press, Berkeley, 1978.

——, *General Economic History*, Collier Books, New York, [1922] 1961.

——, *Roscher and Knies: The Logical Problems of Historical Economics* (tr. Guy Oakes), The Free Press, New York, 1975.

——, *The Methodology of the Social Sciences*, Edward Shils and Henry Finch (eds.), Free Press, New York, 1949.

——, *The Protestant Ethic and the Spirit of Capitalism*, Scribner's, New York, (1904-5) 1958.

——, *The Theory of Social and Economic Organisation* (Translated and edited by A.M. Henderson and Talcott Parsons), Free Press, Glencoe, 1964.

Wiley, Thomas E., *Back to Kant: The Revival of Kantianism in German Social and Historical Thought, 1860-1914*, Wayne State University Press, Detroit.

Bibliography

Abraham, Francis and J.H. Morgan, *Sociological Thought From Comte to Sorokin*, Macmillan India, Chennai, 1985.

Abraham, Francis M., *Modern Sociological Theory: An Introduction*, Oxford University Press, Calcutta, 2000.

Abraham, J.H., *Origins and Growth of Sociology*, Penguin Books, New York, 1977.

Alexander, Jeffrey, *Theoretical Logic in Sociology*, vol. 1, *Positivism, Presuppositions, and Current Controversies*, University of California Press, Berkeley, 1982.

——, 'The "Individualist Dilemma" in Phenomenology and Interactionism' in S.N. Eisenstadt and H.J. Helle (eds.), *Macro-Sociological Theory*, vol. 1, Sage, London, 1985.

Alexander, Jeffrey, and Paul Colomy, 'Toward Neofunctionalism', *Sociological Theory*, 3, 1985.

Althusser, Louis, *For Marx*, Penguin, Harmondsworth, England, 1969.

——, *Politics and History*, NLB, London, 1977.

Althusser, Louis and Etienne Balibar, *Reading Capital*, New Left Books, London, 1970.

Aron, Raymond, *Main Currents in Sociological Thought*, vol. I., Penguin Books, USA, 1965.

——, *German Sociology* (trans. Mary and Thomas Bottormore), Free Press, New York, 1967.

——, *Main Currents in Sociological Thought*, vol. 2, Doubleday, Garden City, 1970.

Bales, Robert Freed, *Interaction Process Analysis*, Mass: Addison-Wesley, Cambridge, 1950.

——, 'Neo-Kantianism', *The Encyclopedia of Philosophy*, vol. 5, Macmillan, New York, 1967.

Benedix, Reinhard and Seymour Martin Lipset, *Class, Status, and Power*, Free Press, New York, 1966.

Benton, Ted, *The Rise and Fall of Structural Marxism: Althusser and his Influence*, St. Martin's, New York, 1984.

Berger, Peter L. and Thomas Luckmann, *The Social Construction of Reality*, Doubleday and Co., Inc., New York, 1967.

Berger, Peter L., *The Sacred Canopy*, Doubleday, New York, 1969.

Bierstedt, Robert, *The Social Order*, McGraw-Hill, Inc., New York, 1974.

——, *American Sociological Theory: A Critical History*, Academic Press, London, 1981.

Black, Max, 'Review of Social Theories of Talcott Parsons', *Journal of Philosophy*, 59, 29 March 1962.

Bleicher, Josef (ed.), *Contemporary Hermeneutics: Hermeneutics as Method, Philosophy and Critique*, Routledge and Kegan Paul, London, 1980.

Blumer, Herbert, 'Society as Symbolic Interaction', in A. Ross (ed.), *Human Behaviour and Social Process*, Houghton Mifflin, Boston, 1962.

Bottomore, T.B., '"Karl Mark": Sociologist or Marxist?' in *Theories and Paradigms in Contemporary Sociology*, Serge Denisoff et al. (ed.), F.E. Peacock Publishers, Inc., Itasca, 1974.

——, *Sociology: A Guide to Problems and Literature*, Blackie and Son (India) Ltd., Bombay 1975.

——, *Marxist Sociology, Macmillan*, London, 1975.

——, 'Out of this World', *New York Review of Books*, 6 November 1969.

Bruun, H.H., *Science, Values and Politics in Max Weber's Methodology*, Munksgaard, Copenhagen, 1972.

Burger, Thomas, *Max Weber's Theory of Concept Formation: History, Laws, and Ideal Types*, Duke University Press, Durham, 1976.

Cicourel, Aron V., *Cognitive Sociology*, Macmillan, London, 1973.

Cohen, G.A., *Karl Marx's Theory of History*, Princeton University Press, New Jersey, 1978.

Colletti, Locio, *Marxism and Hegel*, Verso, London, 1979.

Collins, Randall and Michael Makowsky, *The Discovery of Society*, Random House, New York, 1972.

Comte, Auguste, *Course de Philosophic Positive* (The Course of Positivist Philosophy or the Positive Philosophy), translated and condensed by Harriet Martineau, Trubner, London, 1853.

——, *System de Politique Positive* (System of Positive Polity or Positive Polity), vol. 4, Cress, Paris, 1912.

Coser, Lewis A. (ed.), *The Idea of Social Structure: Papers in Honour of Robert K. Merton*, Harcourt Brace Jovanovich, New York, 1975.

——, *Masters of Sociological Thought*, Rawat Publications, Jaipur, 1997.

Craib, Ian, *Classical Social Theory: An Introduction to the Thought of Marx, Weber, Durkheim, and Simmel*, Oxford University Press, New York, 1997.

Cuff, E.C., W.W. Sharrock and D.W. Francis, *Perspectives in Sociology*, Unwin Hyman, London, 1990.

Durkheim, E., *The Rules of Sociological Method*, Free Press, New York, 1938 [1895].

——, *Suicide*, Free Press, New York, 1951 [1897].

——, *The Division of Labour in Society*, The Free Press, Glencoe: New York, 1964.

——, *The Elementary Forms of Religious Life*, Free Press, New York 1965 [1912].

Ellwood, C.A., *A History of Social Philosophy*, 1955.

Engels, Friedrich, *Anti Duhring*, Foreign Language Press, Peking, 1976 [1878].

Frank, R.I., Translator's introduction to Max Weber, *The Agrarian Sociology of Ancient Civilisations*, NLB, London, 1976.

Giddens, Anthony, *Capitalism and Modern Social Theory*, Cambridge University Press, Cambridge, 1971.

——, *New Rules of Sociological Method: A Positive Critique of Interpretive Sociologies*, Basic Books, New York, 1976.

——, *A Contemporary Critique of Historical Materialism*, Macmillan, London, 1981.

——, *The Constitution of Society: Outline of the Theory of Structuration*, University of California Press, Berkeley, 1984.

——, *The Consequences of Modernity*, Polity Press, Cambridge, 1990.

——, *Sociology*, 4th Edition, Polity Press, Oxford, 2004.

Habermas, Jurgen, *Toward a Rational Society*, Beacon Press, Boston, 1970.

Handel, Warren H., *Contemporary Sociological Theory*, Prentice-Hall, Englewood Cliffs, New Jersey, 1993.

Haralambos, M, *Sociology: Themes and Perspectives*, Oxford University Press, New Delhi, 1999.

Hearn, F., *Reason and Freedom in Sociological Thought*, Allen and Unwin, Boston, 1985.

Hegel, G.W.F., *Philosophy of Right*, Clarendon Press, Oxford, 1958.

Heritage, John, *Garfinkel and Ethnomethodology*, Polity Press, Cambridge, 1984.

Howe, Irving (ed.), *Essential Works of Socialism*, Rinehart and Winston, New York, 1971.

Husserl, Edmund, *Ideas: General Introduction to Pure Phenomenology* (trans. W.R. Boyce Gibson), Humanities Press, New York, 1931.

Johnson, Benton, *Functionalism in Modern Sociology: Understanding Talcott Parsons*, NJ: General Learning Press, Morristown, 1975.

Jordan, Z.A., *The Evolution of Dialectical Materialism*, St. Martin's Press, New York, 1967.

Kalberg, Stephen, 'Max Weber's Types of Rationality: Cornerstones for the Analysis of Rationalisation Process in History', *American Journal of Sociology*, 85, 1980.

Larson, Calvin J., *Major Themes in Sociological Theory*, David Mckay, New York, 1973.

Lefebvre, Henri, *The Sociology of Marx*, Vintage, New York, 1981.

Loomis, Charles and Zona K. Loomis, *Modern Social Theories*, D. Van Nostrand Company, Princeton, 1965.

Lukacs, George, *History and Class Consciousness*, MIT Press, New York, 1968 [1922].

Lukes, S., *Emile Durkheim: His Life and Work*, Standard University Press, Standford, 1973.

Manning Phil, 'Drama as Life: The Significance of Goffman's Changing use of the Theatrical Metaphor', in *The Classical Tradition in Sociology: The American Tradition*, Jeffrey Alexander, Raymond Boudon and Mohamed Cherkaoui (eds.), vol. IV, Sage Publication, London, 1997.

Marx, Karl, *Early Writings*, translated and edited by T.B. Bottomore, McGraw-Hill, New York, 1964.

——, *Selected Writings in Sociology and Social Philosophy*, translated by T.B. Bottomore, McGraw-Hill, London, 1964.

——, *The Economic and Philosophic Manuscripts of 1844*, International Publishers, New York, 1964 [1932].

——, *A Critique of Hegel's Philosophy of Right*, J O'Malley (ed.), Cambridge University Press, 1970 [1843].

——, *Capital*, Lawrence and Wishart, London, 1970.

——, *Grundrisse: Foundations of the Critique of Political Economy*, Middle Sex, Penguin, England, 1973 [1953].

——, *A Contribution to the Critique of Political Economy*, Progress Publishers, Moscow, 1977 [1859].

Marx, Karl and F. Engels, *The German Ideology*, International Publishers, New York, 1947 [1846].

——, *The Holy Family, or Critique of Critical Criticism*, Progress Publishers, Moscow, 1956 [1845].

——, 'The Class Struggle', in *Social Change*, Amitai Etzioni and Eva Etzioni-Halevy (eds.), Basic Books, New York, 1973.

——, *Collected Works*, International Publishers, New York, 1975.

Meek, R., *Studies in the Labour Theory of Value*, Lawrence & Wishart, London, 1973.

Mehan, Hugh and Houston Wood, *The Reality of Ethnomethodology*, Wiley, New York, 1975.

Mitchel, G. Duncan (ed.), *A New Dictionary of Sociology*, Routledge, London, 1999.

Morrison, Ken, *Marx, Durkheim, Weber: Formation of Modern Social Thought*, Sage Publication, London, 1995.

Mueller-Vollmer, Kurt, 'Language, Mind and Artifact: An Outline of Hermeneutic Theory Since the Enlightenment' in *The Hermeneutics Reader*, K. Muller-Vollmer (ed.) Continuum, New York.

Orru, Marco, *Review of Talcott Parsons: On Economy and Society* (by Robert J. Holton and Bryan S. Turner) and *The Integration of Economic and Sociological Theory*, The Marshall Lectures, University of Cambridge, 1953.

Peel, J.D.Y., *Herbert Spencer: The Evolution of a Sociologist*, Heinemann, London, 1971.

Pope, Whitney, *Durkheim's Suicide: A Classic Analysed*, University of Chicago Press, Chicago, 1976.

Rex, John, *Key Problems in Sociological Theory*, Routledge and Kegan Paul, London, 1961.

Ricardo, D., *On the Principles of Political Economy and Taxation*, Batoche Books Kitchener, Canada 2001 [1817].

Rickert, Heinrich, *Science and History: A Critique of Positivist Epistemology* (trans. George Reisman), D. Van Nostrand, Princeton, 1962.

Ritzer, George, *Sociological Theory*, McGraw-Hill Company, Singapore, 1988.

——, *Postmodern Social Theory*, McGraw-Hill, New York, 1997.

Robey, David (ed.), *Structuralism: An Introduction*, Oxford University Press, Oxford, 1973.

Rossides, Daniel W., *The History and Nature of Sociological Theory*, Houghton Mifflin Company, Boston, 1978.

Rotenstreich, Nathan, *Basic Problems of Marx's Philosophy*, Bobb Merrill, Indianapolis, 1965.

Rubel, M., and M. Manale, *Marx Without Myth: A Chronological Study of His Life and Work*, Harper & Row, 1975.

Scruton, R., *A Dictionary of Political Thought*, Pan Books, London, 1982.

Shills, Edward A., Robert Freed Bales and Talcott Parsons, *Working Papers in the Theory of Action*, Free Press, New York, 1953.

Smith A., *The Wealth of Nations*. W. Strahan and T. Cadell, London, 1776.

Spencer, Herbert, *The Principles of Ethics*, (2 vols.), Appleton, New York, 1914 [1892-93].

——, 'The Development Hypothesis', in *Essays: Scientific, Political and Speculative*, vol. 1, Appleton, New York, 1915 [1852].

——, 'Progress: Its Law and Cause', in *Essays: Scientific, Political, and Speculative*, vol. 1, Appleton, New York, 1915 [1857].

——, 'The Development Hypothesis', vol. 1 in *Essays: Scientific, Political and Speculative*, Appleton, New York, 1915 [1852].

——, 'The Social Organism', in *Essays: Scientific, Political and Speculative*, vol. II, Appleton, New York, 1915 [1857].

——, *The Principles of Sociology*, (3 vols.), Appleton, New York, 1925-9 [1876-1896].

——, *An Autobiography*, (2 vols.), Watts, London, 1926 [1904].

——, *The Man Versus the State*, 2nd edn., Watts, London, 1950 [1884].

——, *Social Statics: The Conditions of Human Happiness Specified, and the First of them Developed*, Routledge, London, 1954 [1850].

——, *First Principles*, Dewitt Revolving Fund, New York, 1958 [1862].

——, *The Study of Sociology*, University of Michigan Press, Ann Arbor, 1961 [1873].

——, *Education: Intellectual, Moral, and Physical*, Littlefield, Paterson, N.J. 1963 [1854-1859].

Thompson, K. and J. Junstall (eds.), *Sociological Perspectives, Penguin Books*, Middle-Sex.

Timasheff, Nicholas, S., *Sociological Theory: Its Nature and Growth*, 3rd edn., Random House, New York, 1967.

Tribe, Keith (ed.), *Reading Weber*, Routledge, London, 1989.

Troeltch, Ernst, *The Social Teaching of the Christian Churches*, Allen and Unwin, London, 1956.

Tucker, R.C., *Marx-Engels Reader*, W. W. Norton, New York, 1978.

Wallace, Ruth A. and Alison Wolf, *Contemporary Sociological Theory: Continuing the Classical Tradition*, Prentice-Hall, Inc., Englewood Cliffs, New Jersey, 1980.

Weber, Marianne, *Max Weber: A Biography*, John Wiley & Sons, New York, 1975.

Weber, Max, *The Theory of Social and Economic Organisation*, Oxford University Press, London & New York, 1947.

——, 'Objectivity in Social Science and Social Policy', in *Max Weber: The Methodology of the Social Sciences*, E.A. Shills and H. Finch (eds.), The Free Press, New York, 1949.

——, *The Methodology of the Social Sciences* (trans. and ed. Edward A. Shills and Henry A. Finch), Free Press, Chicago, 1949.

——, *The Protestant Ethic and the Spirit of Capitalism*, Scribner's, New York, 1958 [1904-1905].

——, *General Economic History*, Collier Books, New York, 1961 [1922].

——, *The Theory of Social and Economic Organisation* (trans. and edited by A.M. Henderson and Talcott Parsons), Free Press, Glencoe, 1964.

——, *Economy and Society* (3 vols.) Bedminster Press, Totowa, N.J., 1968 [1921].

——, *Roscher and Knies: The Logical Problems of Historical Economics* (trans. Guy Oakes), The Free Press, New York, 1975.

——, *Economy and Society*, G. Roth and C. Wittich (eds.), University of California Press, Berkeley, 1978.

Weigert, Andrew, *Sociology of Everyday Life*, Longman, New York, 1981.

Wiley, Thomas E., *Back to Kant: The Revival of Kantianism in German Social and Historical Thought*, 1860-1914, Wayne State University Press, Detroit, 1978.

Wilson, Thomas P., 'Normative and Interpretive Paradigms in Sociology' in Jack Douglas (ed.), *Understanding Everyday Life*, Aldine, Chicago, 1970.

Wiltshire, David, *The Social and Political Thought of Herbert Spencer*, Oxford Historical Monograph, Oxford University Press, Oxford, 1978.

Index

9789360803292